Developing Effective Instructional Systems

Developing Effective Instructional Systems

By

Rick Coger, Ph.D.

Assistant Director and Instructional Systems Designer
Regional Medical Education Center, Veterans
Administration Hospitals, St. Louis, Mo. 63125

THE CHRISTOPHER PUBLISHING HOUSE
NORTH QUINCY, MASS. 02171

PRINTED IN

THE UNITED STATES OF AMERICA

To my wife, Lillian, whose loving concern and continuous encouragement to complete this book have caused me to spend many hours of research and writing which otherwise could have been spent with her.

To my son, Brenton, who made it difficult for me to write this book.

To my mother and father, as a small down payment on a large debt.

To my eight brothers and sisters, who deserve special recognition.

Preface

This book is written to assist prospective and practicing teachers in becoming more aware of the broad range and the interrelatedness of the components of instructional systems. It is designed to be used also as a supplementary text for most courses in education (for example: testing and evaluation, educational methods, educational administration, educational psychology, and psychology of learning). Instructional designers, curriculum and subject matter planners, learning theorists, testing and evaluation specialists, administrators, media specialists, members of the school board, parents, and researchers should find this book to be of value.

This book represents an effort to assist teachers in:

1. Selecting instructional systems.
2. Determining the appropriateness of the selected systems.
3. Determining the practicability of the appropriate systems.
4. Evaluating the practical systems.
5. Making decisions about the effectiveness of the utilization of instructional systems.

I am indebted to the following schools, colleges, and universities for permitting me to practice developing instructional systems over a span of thirteen years: Beach Junior High School, Savannah, Georgia; Belize Technical College and St. John's College, Belize City, Belize, Central America; Ball State University, Muncie, Indiana; The Ohio State University, Columbus, Ohio; Central State University and Wilberforce University, Wilberforce, Ohio.

My appreciation is expressed to: Ball State University Teacher's College Alumni Association, whose small grant served as a catalyst in producing this book; my colleagues Ermin Frey and Bragge Kristensen for their guidance; Jeanette O'Neal, Joan Holley and Coleen Cosby for their efforts to produce the typed materials; and to all my former students.

Rick Coger
4332 Chateau de Ville Drive
St. Louis, Missouri 63129

Contents

Introduction

The days of poorly designed materials for teaching are numbered. It is no longer necessary to do without some form of specifications and quality control in education. If all instructional components are selected and designed on the basis of objectives, presentation form, subject content and student characteristics, if all media, methods, and instructional events are put together because they are the most appropriate for each objective and for each general and specific goal, and if the interrelated combination is thoroughly validated, an instructional system exists.

A system as used in this writing denotes the state or condition of harmonious and orderly relationship. It is a group of interacting interrelated and/or interdependent elements forming a collective entity. An instructional system is broadly concerned with all elements of instruction. It is oriented toward the inputs, processes and outputs of the instructional process. There are ten necessary elements in a system. They are:

1. Function (Purpose)
2. Input (Resources)
3. Sequence (Process)
4. Output (Result)
5. Environment—Physical, Social, Emotional and Mental.
6. Human Agent—(System designer, system engineer, system manager, system analyst, the executor, etc.)
7. Boundary (Inclusion in or exclusion from a line or area.)
8. Feedback (The observed functions of outputs.)
9. Signal (Communication, information)
10. Noise (Distraction)

An instructional system is a planned, validated selection

of media, methods, equipment, facilities, teachers, students, and supportive services used in performing activities to achieve the objectives of instruction. The Commission on Instructional Technology defined an instructional system as a systematic way of designing, carrying out, and evaluating the total process of learning and teaching in terms of objectives in hopes of bringing about more effective instruction.

Effectiveness is the measurement of the performance of students in relation to the system used. This measurement is the ratio of the number of objectives a student achieved to the time he took to achieve them.

The level of effectiveness of an instructional system is identified by:

> What is taught?
> How?
> To Whom?
> Through what means?
> In what sort of environment?
> With what effects?

The concepts of senses and learning are very important in instructional systems. Research indicated that we learn about 1 percent through taste, 1½ percent through the sense of touch, 3½ percent through the sense of smell, 11 percent through hearing and 83 percent through visual experiences.

Retention of what is learned is also related to the experiences of the senses. Research indicates that we generally remember:

> 10 percent of what we *read*;
> 20 percent of what we *hear*;
> 30 percent of what we *see*;
> 50 percent of what we *hear and see*;
> 70 percent of what we *say*; and
> 90 percent of what we *say* as we *do* a thing.

The inferences one may make from this information will vary. So should the instructional systems of a given teacher in one teaching situation in contrast to another. Instructional systems, all parts which have specific relationships to each other and to the total systems, are the main means by which performance specifications and quality control will reach the classroom and the students.

In designing an instructional system one should:

1. Analyze the problem;
2. Define the objective;
3. Select the teaching strategies;
4. Try out, evaluate, revise, and recycle the teaching strategies.

Keep in mind as you read this book that:

1. Each learner is unique;
2. Perception is the foundation of learning;
3. The learner must become involved;
4. Learning experiences must be suitable;
5. Teaching strategies must be appropriate;
6. Creativity is the goal of learning.

Manner of Teaching

Teaching is the promotion of achievement of learners. It should be practiced in such a manner whereas the intellectual integrity and the capacity for independent judgment of learners are respected.

Some educators have defined teaching as being an *Art* — "good teaching is caught and not taught." Some others defined teaching as being a *Science* —"good teaching is taught and not caught." This book emphasized the latter. However, some research has indicated that effective teaching is a combination of both. "Good" teaching is somewhere on the line of continuum between the two poles — an art and a science.

Some activities that teachers perform are vital to their jobs but not to the act of teaching. Activities related to the act of teaching are divided into two categories, *logical acts* and *strategic acts*. Other activities are called *institutional acts*.

Logical Acts	*Strategic Acts*	*Institutional Acts*
1. Deducing	Questioning	Taking roll
2. Concluding	Motivating	Making reports
3. Explaining	Evaluating	Chaperoning dances
4. Comparing	Testing	Attending faculty meetings
5. Defining	Reinforcing	Patrolling halls, playgrounds & cafeteria
6. Justifying	Encouraging	Collecting money
7.	Trusting	Serving as a committee member
8.	Respecting	
9.	Measuring	
10.	Advising	

The Elements of an Instructional System

The model illustrates the components of an instructional system and the relationships each component has to the others. The system itself is examined in the nine chapters that follow. It may have irrelevant features for a given system. Or it may demand measures from the users that cannot be obtained. Adapt the components that fit your needs. This model should not limit one's instruction but improve it. It cannot insure results. Only the teacher can do that. It will help the teacher in obtaining desired results. (See Figure 1 on page 16.)

Will This Book Help You?

At the beginning of each chapter some questions are presented. These questions will help you to identify the major problem area the chapter covers.

At the end of each chapter, except for chapters 8 and 9, you will find examples selected from representative subject fields. These will illustrate each step of the instructional plan. The topics are listed on the facing page.

Subject Area	Unit	Topic	Level
1. History	Early U. S. History	The Revolutionary War	6th Grade
2. Music	Instrumental Music	Writing Harmony	9-10th Grades
3. General Science	Weather	Air Masses	Jr. High School
4. Language Arts	Poetry	Rustic Poetry	5-6th Grades
5. Mathematics	Fractions	Percents & Fractions	Jr. High School
6. Psychology	Perception	Self-Fulfilling Prophecy	Teacher Education (College)

Worksheets are located after each sample topic. They should be used in designing your instruction systems. This book is not designed "to teach" or treat in detail all the topics mentioned. You are encouraged to examine references and to have them at hand while designing your systems.

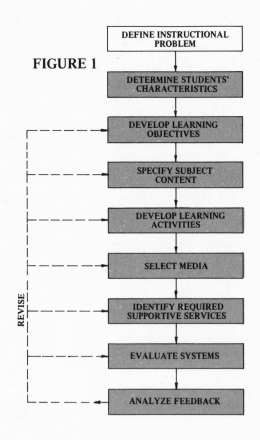

FIGURE 1

Chapter 1

Define Instructional Problem

... What problems do you want to solve in teaching a topic?
... What are the desired competencies of the learner?

One of the most realistic means of defining the instructional problem is to do so in terms of the desired competencies of the student. By listing desired competencies as a delineation of the problem, the teacher will recognize the solution by an assessment of the student's knowledge as demonstrated under actual classroom situations in the form of competencies. Thus a student may be asked to take tests (oral or written) to prove the desired competencies in a given subject. If the student is successful on the tests, the instructional problem is solved.

The competency-based approach to learning and instruction is an alternative to some of the more customary approaches. This approach demands mastery learning on the

17

part of the student. The majority of the responsibilities for learning is placed on the student. The premise is that the student learns from his own behavior and not necessarily from the behavior of the teacher. This approach requires students to take the initiative and to perform so that competencies can be noted or not noted.

A committee appointed by the U. S. Office of Education has published a book called *The Power of Competency-Based Teacher Education.* This book provides invaluable insights and ideas for competency-based education.

If the problem is defined adequately in the form of desired competencies of students the teacher will encounter fewer problems in specifying learning objectives. This serves as a prerequisite for all other components in designing an instructional system. It is, likewise, one of the most important components in the system.

A system exists because a set of entities together with their properties serves a need. The need may be real or imaginary. The need is the problem that the system solves, or attempts to solve.

Before a system can be developed to serve a need, the problem should be identified. Simply identify what must be done. Identify what you want to accomplish in teaching a topic.

The problem may be broad or narrow in scope. Some broad-type problems are: "Prepare students to be good citizens" — a societal-determined problem; "Increase the vocational competency of students"; and "Develop desirable leisure-time interests." Some examples of problems stated more specifically are: "To accept the responsibilities of not defacing classroom furniture"; "To develop competencies in communicating in the Spanish language"; "To conjugate verbs properly"; and "To recite Jean Piaget's theory of intellectual development."

The problem may be a consideration of a social, physical, emotional, mental, biological, ethical or philosophical need. The need may be derived from the demands or wishes of the school, community, society or some other element within the boundary of the system.

Identifying the problem or competency is the beginning of the process of designing an instructional system. The process begins with the teacher. The teacher is the director or facilitator of learning experiences. As a manager of a baseball team platoons players to win games, so the teacher calls upon the spectrum of resources available to solve an instructional problem.

However, it is not sufficient for the teachers to merely use learning resources. They must above all be able to identify and define the instructional problem.

Defining instructional problems will vary from subject to subject, from school to school, from grade to grade, and from class to class. This element cannot be treated within the scope of this book.

In summary, defining the instructional problem involves:

1. Listing and analyzing the learning needs of students;
2. Listing the desired competencies students should have;
3. Listing the principles and concepts that will be used to solve the learning needs of students.

Planning for instruction starts, then, with defining the instructional problems. Here are some examples as applied to the sample topics.

History—To stress the fact that the American Revolutionary War produced a major crisis in the history of Great Britain. It was the beginning of the history of a new nation. This influential event in world history changed the order of the Western world.

Music—To stress that the sound of musical instruments is the result of a variety of components based on a fundamental tone called harmonics. Their frequencies are in a simple mathematical relationship to each other. Although the volume, pitch and timbre of a tone are subject to the laws of acoustics, the quality of a tone is a matter of aesthetic concern.

General Science—To stress that weather forecasting is often predicted from local observations. The type of clouds, and the light coming from them, and the direction and strength of the wind are observed. Successive readings of the barometer are read also.

Language Arts—To stress the development of an appreciation for rustic poetry.

Mathematics—To stress that the heart of arithmetic is a system of numbers. The sets of numbers used are generally the positive integers and zero; positive common and decimal fractions; and combinations of the two, known as mixed numbers.

Psychology—To stress that the psychology of perception emphasizes internal, psychological forces such as needs, wants, values, anxieties, attitudes and interests.

WORKSHEET

Define Instructional Problem
(Desired competencies and needs analysis)

1.

2.

3.

4.

5.

6.

7.

8.

9.

10.

11.

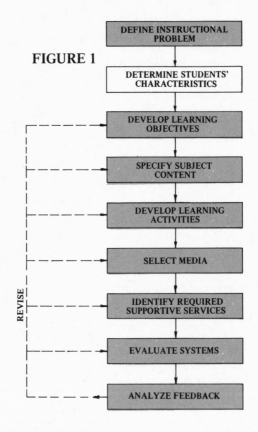

FIGURE 1

Chapter 2

Determine Students' Characteristics

... What are some known factors about student, or groups of students which will affect plans for their learning?

... Do the students have the background preparation to study the unit or course, or are they already proficient in what will be taught?

A teacher once began a course by giving the final examination which was used in the same course the previous term. Unexpectedly, more than half the class passed the examination! Another teacher began a course by giving the final examination which was used in the same course the previous term. No student passed the examination. At the end of the course, the same examination was administered. Unexpectedly, no student passed the examination.

The above examples indicate that both teachers needed

to know what each student brought to class and took away. The reasons for the results observed by both teachers are many. In the first example, some reasons may be that the students knew a considerable amount of the course content before taking the course; the student had prior knowledge of the questions; the test was badly constructed; or, the test was administered improperly. In the second case, some reasons might be as follows. The questions had a high index of difficulty or discrimination; students have problems in reading or comprehension; the teaching strategies were executed poorly; the test was not culturally fair; or the test was improperly scored.

Knowledge of the student's characteristics will give the teacher some clues about the student's entering behavior to the unit of instruction or course. The entering behavior refers to prerequisites. A student who is learning to find quotients for long division problems must possess entering behaviors which include, among others, the ability to subtract and multiply. Before a student can spell words orally, he must possess the ability to name the letters of the alphabet.

There are many things a teacher can do to learn more about the background of students. Some are:

1. Administer a prerequisite test (pre-test) — oral or written.
2. Administer a pre-topic questionnaire — oral or written. Example: "How many of you have ever used a slide rule?"
3. Investigate the student's cumulative record.
4. Consult counselors, advisors and other teachers.
5. Investigate test results on units and courses of students related to the one you are about to teach.
6. Visit students at home.

Student characteristics will affect the teacher's decisions concerning the selection of learning objectives, level at which to start a unit or course, depth of treatment, media utilization, required supportive services, and the variety and extent of learning activities to be planned. The reason for this

analysis is to determine, as accurately as possible, the current ability and achievement level of each student. This information will assist in designing appropriate instruction for each student or group of students who require a given treatment and spare the boredom and waste of time caused by unneeded or inappropriate instruction. Some factors, as the following, might be taken into consideration.

1. Reading ability level.
2. Physical characteristics.
3. Social characteristics.
4. Emotional characteristics.
5. Mental characteristics.
6. Cross cultures.
7. Similar culture.
8. Sex.
9. Geographical location.
10. Chronological age.
11. Race.
12. Socio-economic background.
13. Religion.
14. Language.
15. Dialect.
16. Political ideology.
17. Environmental limitations.
18. Attention span.
19. Study habits.
20. Motivation and interest in subject matter.
21. I. Q. and other measures of intelligence.
22. Results of achievement and aptitude tests in the given subject.
23. Grade level.
24. Related experiences.

Make a list of all pertinent data and information about students and keep it before you for reference as you proceed to the subsequent planning stages. Here are examples of *student characteristics* as applied to the problem (Topics) identified at the end of chapter 1.

History

Reading ability range: 2.9 to 4.6

Some physical characteristics: Some of the girls have reached the stage of puberty; students are extremely active; students become fatigued easily as a result of mental and physical exertion; it is difficult for many of the students to manipulate a pencil.

Grade level: 30 sixth graders.

Socio-economic background: Rural community in cotton, vegetable and fruit growing region. Many of the parents work as pickers and packers.

Music

Chronological ages: 14.1 to 16.4

I. Q. range: 82 to 139

Related experiences: All students have written a two-part harmony instrumental.

Religion: Most of the students are Roman Catholics.

General Science

Language: 80 percent of the students speak Spanish.

Attention span: Very short; students need to be challenged with a mixture of group and individualized activities.

Social Characteristics: Students quarrel among themselves frequently; competition is noticeable; peer group is powerful; the interest of the boys and girls are divergent.

Race: 75 percent of the students are Mexican American.

Language Arts

Mental age range: 4.1 to 5.3

Motivation and interest in subject area: The topic of Rustic Poetry was considered for class study after much interest was shown in student report on Robert Frost.

Study habits: Students take pride in completing classwork and homework on schedule.

Emotional characteristics: Students express their emotions freely and openly; they are sensitive to criticism and ridicule and have difficulty adjusting to failure; they are eager to please the teacher.

Mathematics

Sex: All 12 students are males.

Culture: Students seem to have similar cultural backgrounds.

Dialect: Students' dialect differs from that of the teacher.

Mental characteristics: Students are highly skillful with usages of language; they are highly imaginative and inventive; they are eager to learn; they have much more facility in speech than in writing; they tend to set unrealistically high standards for themselves and tend to be perfectionists; they comprehend abstract concepts well.

Psychology

Students' interest: Most of the students do not expect to go to graduate school.

Geographical location: Southwestern and rural in the state of Ohio.

Political ideology: The community is considered to be highly conservative.

Environmental ideology: Students have negative attitude toward school, they have poor health, inadequate diet, limited language and reading skills and poor estimate of themselves; they show interest in the practical as opposed to the abstract and have preference for physical rather than verbal learning; they have been victimized by overt discrimination in the form of older school buildings and tests, poorer teachers and higher teacher turnovers.

WORKSHEET

Determine students' characteristics (what factors are known about the student group, or individual students, which will affect plans for their learning?).

1.

2.

3.

4.

5.

6.

7.

WORKSHEET

8.

9.

10.

11.

12.

13.

14.

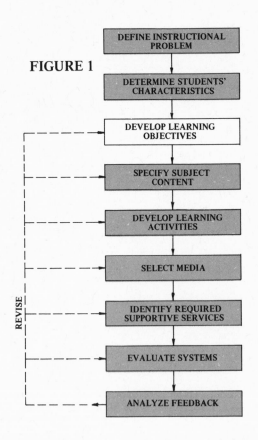

FIGURE 1

Chapter 3

Develop Learning Objectives

. . . What should the students know, be able to do, or in what ways should they behave differently after completing a prescribed unit or course of instruction?

If students are not sure where they are going, they are liable to end up anywhere. Objectives specifying learning should be written to inform students what they are expected to learn. Objectives serve as guides for teachers. An objective is a statement that describes in observable and measurable terms the expected output performance of the product of the instructional system. If the objectives are stated clearly, monitoring the instructional system for quality control can be a reality. Each objective should be directly linked to the concept or attitude stated in the definition of the instructional problem.

Writing learning objectives are difficult but essential. Some teachers write their objectives immediately after they have defined the problem, some others write them only after the subject content is outlined; and others write them after the learning activities have been selected. Sequentially, writing objectives after the problem has been defined is recommended but in actual practice it does not always work.

Writing objectives is a developmental activity that requires changes, additions and refinements as one enters subsequent planning steps. It is recommended to start with loosely worded objectives, move ahead in the planning sequence, and return to spell out the objectives in detail as each one becomes more evident.

Some of the strongest reasons for using learning objectives are listed below.

1. Through clear objectives, teachers are able to tell other teachers what they teach.
2. Students and their advisors are able to plan their course programs better when they can read course descriptions that include objectives.
3. Objectives are vital entities in an accountability-based educational system.
4. Objectives specify to students what is to be learned and how they are to demonstrate learning.
5. Curriculum planners are better able to arrange sequences of courses or units of instruction when objectives are given.
6. Objectives stated in performance standards can help teachers determine the adequacy of their instructional system.
7. Because objectives include performance standards, they represent a minimal level of performance to be sought by all, or most students.
8. Objectives are necessary when evaluating students using the competency-based approach.
9. Objectives are necessary as guides in evaluating the effectiveness of instructional systems.
10. Teachers and administrators can determine the level of objectives in terms of categories—cognitive, psychomotor or affective.

Below are two objectives. The first is not a learning objective, while the second one is.

1. The student will know what factors led to the American Revolutionary War.
2. The student will list and describe in writing at least four factors that gave rise to the American Revolutionary War, as shown in the textbook.

The second objective informs students what they are to do to demonstrate that learning has occurred. The first objective lacks specificity; it does not indicate how the students are to demonstrate what they know and to what extent they know the required information.

In writing objectives, behavior means actions and movements that one can be observed making (e.g., seeing, hearing or feeling). All objectives require a psychomotor component.

Performance refers to the result of the learners' action that is evaluated to see whether they have successfully completed an objective. Product is frequently used as a synonym for performance.

Now that some of the basic terms have been reviewed, we will analyze the components of the objectives. Objectives should contain the following five elements:

1. *The Actual Behavior* to be employed in demonstrating mastery of the learning objective. This component specifies observable acts or behaviors that the learner is to perform. The selection of appropriate action verbs, to describe the required student behavior, is a difficult part of writing objectives. Here is a general list of action *verbs* often used:

apply	arrange	build	compare
contrast	define	demonstrate	distinguish
describe	construct	duplicate	explain
identify	list	make	name
order	interpret	rank	recall
repeat	show	solve	compute
state	tell	write	match

2. *Who* is to perform the desired behavior.

3. The *relevant conditions* under which the behavior is to be performed.
4. The *result* of the behavior, which will be evaluated to determine whether the objective is mastered.
5. The *standard* that will be used to evaluate the success of the product or performance.

Each of the above components is identified in the objective given below. The number of the component is shown above the portion of the learning objective. No number appears over the words or phrases that is not a part of a specific component.

/"The student [2] // will be able // to spell correctly [1] // 30 [5] out of 40 // words [4] // selected at random from the 300 words listed in the spelling textbook, // during the one-half [3] hour final examination. // The student // will write [1] // the words [4] // as they are presented [3] by the tape recorder. //In order to be correct, the spelling of each [5] word must match those in the spelling textbook." /

Categories of Objectives

It is relevant to examine and illustrate now the three taxonomies of learner behaviors representing the three domains of behavior with which teachers have dealt — cognitive, affective, and psychomotor.

Bloom (1956), Krathwohl (1964), Simpson (1972) and others have prepared taxonomies for the three classes of behavior. These taxonomies represent only broad classifications of human behaviors and objectives. Behavioral taxonomies can be used as guidelines for sequentially arranging objectives according to complexity, difficulty or level. See Appendix D.

A taxonomy is a classification scheme consisting of a comprehensive listing of abilities and behaviors essential in learning. Of the three domains or areas, the one given most attention in schools is the cognitive domain.

The objectives classified as *cognitive* emphasize problem-solving and other intellectual tasks. It is concerned with knowledge, information, and intellectual abilities such as naming, listing, solving, and so on. Behaviors in this domain range from performing simple recall tasks, understanding of principles, concepts, trends, and generalizations to synthesizing bodies of learned information.

A condensed version of the cognitive domain of the taxonomy of objectives is listed below. They are listed in sequential order and indicate the levels of cognitive behaviors under which objectives may be classified.

1. *Knowledge*—involves the recall of specifics, methods, processes, patterns, structure, setting and universals.
2. *Comprehension*—refers to a type of understanding or apprehension such as those involved in translation, interpretation and extrapolation of information.
3. *Application*—represents the use of abstractions in particular and concrete situations.
4. *Analysis*—involves the breakdown of the relative hierarchy of ideas, elements, relationships, and organizations.
5. *Synthesis*—involves putting together pieces, parts, and elements, and arranging and combining them so as to form a whole.
6. *Evaluation*—judgment about the value of materials, processes, and methods for given purposes.

The second domain is called the *affective domain*. It encompasses attitudes, feelings, appreciation, values, beliefs, likes and dislikes. It is the most difficult of the three domains to measure. The following is an abstract of the taxonomy of objectives for the affective domain.

1. *Receiving* (Attending)—at this level the learner should be: sensitized to certain awareness; willing to tolerate and receive a given stimulus; willing to have controlled or selected attention.
2. *Responding*—the compliance, willingness, and satisfaction in responses.
3. *Valuing*—the acceptance, preference, and commitment for a value.

4. *Organization*—the conceptualization and organization of a value system.
5. *Characterization*—the internationalization and generalization of a set of values.

The third and final category is the *psychomotor domain* or motor-skills area. It deals with performance and skills requiring the use and coordination of skeletal muscles, such as manipulating and constructing.

Below is the taxonomy for behaviors in the psychomotor domain.

1. *Perception*—a process of becoming aware of objects, qualities, or relations by sensory stimulation, cue selection, and translation.
2. *Set*—preparatory mental, physical and emotional adjustments and readiness for a particular kind of action or experience.
3. *Guide Response*—an early step in the development of skills promoted by imitation and trial and error.
4. *Mechanism*—learned responses becoming habitual.
5. *Complex Overt Response*—the student can perform a motor act that is considered complex. One should be able to perform the act efficiently and smoothly.
6. *Adaptation*—modifying motor activities to meet the demands of new problematic situations requiring a physical response.
7. *Origination*—using the student's understandings, abilities, and skills developed in the psychomotor domain to create new motor acts or ways of manipulating materials.

Although it is often virtually impossible to isolate the three behavior domains, it is practical to place them in one of the three categories. The above taxonomies are shown in the form of a hierarchy. The lower levels are less complex in nature than related objectives at upper levels. In most cases, those at the upper levels are built on those at the lower levels.

Justification of Objectives

Students often question the merits of much of what they are directed to study. However, some teachers assume that their choice of objectives will be accepted by students without question as being worthwhile and necessary. It is recommended that students be told *why* it is important for them to study a particular objective.

Informing students of objectives, together with a statement of *justification,* can bring about greater student cooperation. The students will know that the teachers are helping them to learn necessary information.

The justification of an objective may not be necessary when the reason for it is obvious or when we can assume that all students will accept it. But in many cases the justification is of real value.

There are many limitations in writing and justifying objectives. Some of these limitations may be avoided by obtaining objectives from one of the many national clearing houses, or from other teachers. Because the development of practical objectives is a difficult and time-consuming task, teachers can now obtain the list of objectives from which they can choose or adapt those which meet their needs.

Learning objectives do not tell teachers how they should teach or what specific instructional methods they should use. Objectives serve as guides for teachers in identifying:

1. What the students are able to do before beginning a unit, topic, or course.
2. What the students should be able to do in instructional units that follow the unit of concern.
3. What the students should be able to do after completing their formal education.
4. The required instructional resources and teacher's capabilities with a given subject.
5. What the student will learn specifically.
6. The domains—cognitive, psychomotor, or affective.

7. The levels of learning.
8. Test items, examination techniques, and evaluation instruments.
9. Information that can be used in comparing and studying educational programs.
10. Some of the principles of ordering human-learning outcomes.

Here are examples of learning objectives from the sample problems identified in chapter 1.

History

Using a 20-minute tape-recorded lecture on "Ten Factors That Led to the Revolutionary War in America," the student will be given forty minutes to write a critique on five of the ten factors given. The product will be evaluated by the extent to which the student employs the evaluative criteria presented in assigned reading and class lectures. *Justification:* There are reasons for all things someone does. The Revolutionary War marked the beginning of a new era in North America.

Music

Given one hour and the use of the textbook the student will write a four harmony instrumental. The standard which will be used to evaluate the success of the product is listed on page 103 of the textbook.

General Science

Given the temperature, humidity, wind direction, visibility, and cloud types, the student will name the air mass with 80 percent accuracy. *Justification:* One is able to identify an air mass by knowing the characteristics that make each air mass unique.

Language Arts

The student will demonstrate the form of rustic poetry by writing one as a home-work assignment. Successful performance will be based on whether the student distinguishes in the poem three characteristics of rustic poetry as shown in the textbook. *Justification:* This will provide the student with a background for understanding and appreciating this form of poetry.

Mathematics

Given ten different percent numbers, the student will change correctly at least nine of those numbers to fractions in an hour.

Psychology

Without the textbook and within ten minutes the student will explain the experiment that led to the phenomenon psychologists call *self-fulfilling prophecy.* Distinguish the four parts of the experiment.

WORKSHEET

Learning Objectives (Identify the domain and levels)	Justifications
1.	1.
2.	2.
3.	3.
4.	4.
5.	5.
6.	6.
7.	7.
8.	8.
9.	9.
10.	10.
11.	11.

WORKSHEET (UNIT PLANNING)

I. Basic Course Information:
   A. Course Title:
   B. Course Number:
   C. Unit or Credit Hours:
   D. Prerequisites:

II. Course Description (Catalog Description):

III. Rationale of The Course (Why Take This Course):

IV. Identify Unit or Topic:

V. Rationale For Unit or Topic:

VI. Instructional Modes (See Appendix B):

VII. Outline of Learning Sequences:
   (Concepts or Principles & Proposed Dates)

   A.

   B

   C.

   D.

   E.

   F.

VIII. Evaluation Procedures:
   A. Grading Policies:
   B. Tests:
   C. Quizzes:
   D. Inventories:

IX. Attendance Policies:

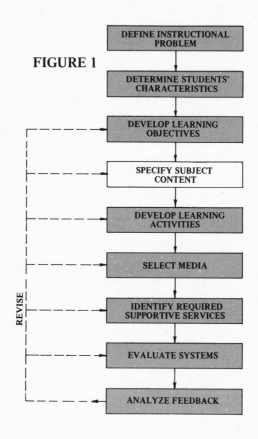

FIGURE 1

Chapter 4

Specify Subject Content

... What subject content is needed to support each objective?

Subject content contains the skills (step-by-step procedures, conditions, and requirements), knowledge (facts, data, and information), and attitudinal factor of any topic. For some teachers, specifying the subject content is the starting point for their instructional systems. This is not recommended as shown in the Introduction. Objectives and subject content are closely related.

Subject contents, like objectives, are generally organized in an order from the simple to the complex. But unlike objectives, subject contents are given in an order from the general to specific and sometimes from the specific to the general. They start from concrete facts, move to concepts, then to principles, and to the more abstract levels.

A sequence of order is desirable with the subject content because certain parts of the content must be mastered as a basis for subsequent learning. It is believed that such a pattern promotes longer retention and easier understanding.

The subject content is a partial fulfillment of the demands of the objective. Or "the objective is what you want the content to do." There is a check-and-balance system involved. The teacher can check the content against the objectives and then proceed to the next step if the confirmation is positive.

The content should be used as the basis for the student's learning experiences. It must support the objectives, students' characteristics, and the instructional problem.

In many instructional systems, the textbook is often the primary instructional resource by which the content is derived. This practice is not recommended. The textbook should be considered as only one resource for selecting subject content. Teachers should use other forms of media. Some examples are: television, film, journals, pamphlets, published curriculums, other teachers and consultants, students, and one's own experiences.

Many people assume that there exist a fixed body of skills, knowledge, and attitudes which all students need to master in order to be educated. They assume that in some way this body of skills, knowledge and attitudes has been defined for teachers. They assume that the subject content is packaged neatly into fixed and established courses of study.

But these assumptions are contradicted by what is known from the study of education. The history of education testifies to constant change in society and education. Change is inescapable and rapid and new social problems, including human survival crises, face mankind, rather than society remaining immobile and changeless.

Consequently, varied body of content and learning experiences are necessary for individuals from a variety of cultural and community backgrounds in a changing world. A fixed body of skills, knowledge and attitudes to be mastered by every person cannot be taught or learned. Experiences and opportunities must change with the growth of knowledge concerning the individual, society, values, and the disciplines. Content cannot stay constant over the years, established and fixed for all learners, in a world in which knowledge explodes.

Below are some examples of *subject content* taken from the same problems.

History
  A. Origins of the Revolution.
    1. Establishment of English Colonies.
    2. The English Ideas of Local Government.
    3. The French and Indian War.
    4. The Seven-Year War.
  B. Immediate Causes of the Conflict.
    1. The Conflict of Interest Between the Colonies and Great Britain.
    2. The Stamp Act.
    3. The Boston Massacre.
    4. The Continental Congress.

Music
  A. Four-part writing.
  B. 1. Soprano.
    2. Alto.
    3. Tenor.
    4. Bass.
  B. Position of Notes.
    1. Fifth.
    2. Third.
    3. Root.

General Science
  A. Definition of an Air Mass: A widespread body of air with similar properties throughout.
  B. General Characteristics of Air Mass:
    1. Tropical—warmer than the land below; high moisture content; poor visibility; stratus clouds; drizzle; dew; mass generally moves east and north.
    2. Polar—colder than the land below; low moisture content; good visibility; cumulus clouds; showers; thunderstorms; mass moves generally east and south.

   C. Designations of Air Masses.
      1. cP—continental Polar.
      2. mP—maritime Polar.
      3. mT—maritime Tropical.

Language Arts
   A. Verification terms.
      1. Couplet.
      2. Doggerel.
      3. Elision.
      4. Fallin Rhythm.
      5. Stanza.
   B. Rustic Poetry by Robert Frost.
      1. "Home Burial."
      2. "The Road Not Taken."
      3. "Mending Wall."
      4. "To a Thinker."
      5. "Fire and Ice."

Mathematics
   A. Percentage.
      1. Meaning of percent.
      2. Types of percentage problems.
   B. Fractions.
      1. Meaning of fractions.
      2. Types of fractions.
         a. improper fractions.
         b. proper fractions.
      3. Addition of fractions.
      4. Subtraction of fractions.
      5. Multiplication of fractions.
      6. Division of fractions.

Psychology
   A. Definition of self-fulfilling prophecy.
   B. Definition of cognitive dissonance, the Hawthorne effect, and the experimenter bias effect.
   C. Test of inflected acquisition.
   D. Pygmalion in the Classroom.
   E. The experimenters Robert Rosenthal and Lenore Jacobson.

WORKSHEET

Specify Subject Content.
(Knowledge, skills and attitudes to be developed in the topic, unit or course.)

A. Knowledge

    1.   4.

    2.   5.

    3.   6.

B. Skills

    1.   4.

    2.   5.

    3.   6.

C. Attitudes

    1.   4.

    2.   5.

    3.   6.

FIGURE 1

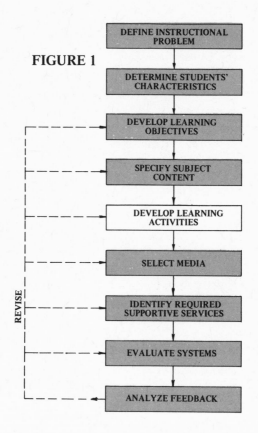

Chapter 5

Develop Learning Activities

. . . What will students do?
. . . What will teachers do?
. . . What activities will be used as the means to achieving the objectives?

There are many roads to learning. Traditionally, the teacher presents the information and the students learn. To achieve learning objectives in today's schools, both the teacher and students undertake a variety of activities. These activities may be classified into three categories: 1. Teacher-student interaction, 2. Independent study, and 3. presentation by the teacher or student wherein he or she alone plans for and communicates to others. All learning-teaching activities are related to one of these categories.

Teacher-Student Interaction

Interaction between teacher and students and among students takes place by means of discussions, reports, projects and the like. Such activities are usually most effective when conducted in relatively small groups to permit discussions, questions, and a free flow of ideas.

The importance of interaction cannot be overemphasized. It promotes activities that permits the teacher and students to review, clarify, correct, reinforce, and apply the learning that has resulted from the presentation sessions or independent studies.

Teacher-student interaction can be of maximum benefits for the following reasons:

1. Students are able to learn from each other as well as from the teacher.
2. Student's understanding of concepts and principles may be tested.
3. Activities may be entirely student directed.
4. The teacher can be a participating member rather than the dominating member of the group.
5. Students are permitted to organize and present their ideas to others.
6. Students can practice leadership.
7. Students can reinforce their own learning by explaining a concept or principle to help other students understand.
8. Students who need encouragement can be recognized.
9. The teacher can become aware of the success or shortcomings of an instructional system.
10. Students who are making inadequate progress can be identified.
11. The teacher will most likely obtain valid suggestions from students for possible revision of various phases of an instructional system.

Independent Study

The framework of independent study is designed for each student to work alone to pursue a goal of learning. Research suggests that learning can best be accomplished by the individual for himself, when the student works at his own rate, is actively involved in performing specific tasks, and has successful results. This suggests a separate set of learning activities for each objective designed for each student according to his individual characteristics.

Independent study features for the student self-responsibility, self-pacing, and successful learning. Some of the terms applied to this pattern are: Self-instruction, individualized learning, individualized prescribed instruction, self-directed study, and independent study.

Resources designed appropriately for students engaged in individual learning activities are numerous. Many approaches to independent study are being explored on various levels in schools throughout the world. The literature contains many articles on these projects. They may give you some ideas or you may review commercial programs.

Presentation by Teacher or Student

This method illustrates a one-way transmission process. The presenter is perhaps at the front of the classroom before a group presenting information, instructions, and interpretations. This role is performed to a group of any size in any subject matter. The presentation process can also take place without the presentor being physically present if it is presented on video tape, film, or the like.

When a presentation is made the learner may be provided with hand-out materials or alike. The student may be directed to take notes during the presentation. In this type of activity, the learner may be active mentally, but generally passive physically.

Most teachers have accepted the fact that learning is an active process and that learning occurs best through the process of doing. Some teachers incorporate active student participation as part of their presentation format by: 1. providing printed outlines and diagrams; 2. directing students to take notes and write critiques; and 3. asking students to respond to questions in a worksheet. Some teachers use simple mechanical-response devices for feedback in their presentation while some of the larger universities use complex electronic equipment to promote active student participation during the presentation.

The assumption is that in the presentation process all students need the same knowledge, skills, and attitudes and that they are acquiring the same understanding, to the same level of comprehension, at the same time. Students are forced to learn in a lock-step manner.

Even though the trend is toward the other two categories, presentations can serve appropriately with the following activities:

1. Demonstrate a skill.
2. Provide orientation to other activities.
3. Discuss objectives.
4. Introduce new topics.
5. Create interest and motivate students in a topic or subject.
6. Provide special enrichment and supplementary materials.
7. Introduce new materials and development on a given problem.
8. Point out special applications of the subject at hand.

The three categories we have examined—teacher-student interaction, independent study and presentation by teacher or student—provide the frame for developing learning activities. They provide the means for obtaining answers to the following questions.

1. Are there experiences that can be served best through one format over another?
2. Is the subject content of such that the student should learn on his own, at his own pace or within a group?
3. Is there a need for private consultation?

An Analysis of the Conditions of Learning

The effective teacher is one who determines the level of the student's development, decides how the student learns best, and help the student to achieve at his own rate. To accomplish these goals the teacher must realize that students are more likely to learn some knowledge, skills and attitudes when they have learned the prerequisite capabilities associated with the learning objective.

Gagné has developed a model designed to show that success in one type of learning is dependent upon prerequisite knowledge of lower types of learning. He proposed eight different types of learning, ranging from the simple to the complex.

One can use Gagné's approach to identify activities that are most relevant to the desired performance of students. If a set of capabilities which the student needs to learn before he can understand a given concept or principle were to be analyzed, the teacher would more likely develop a more effective and viable instructional system.

Gagné's hierarchical model of learning (1965, pp. 58-61) based on a description of types of learning is shown below:

Type 8—Problem Solving - A combination of two or more principles to arrive at a solution; involves thinking skills. Example: A student who understands that round things roll puts a ball in a place where it will not roll away.

Type 7—Principle Learning - A combination of two or more concepts connected in such a way that the student is able to apply what he has learned to a wide variety of similar situations; an acquisition of a clear understanding (not rote memory) of a statement relating to two or more concepts. Example: A student combines the concepts of round and ball when it is learned that round things roll.

Type 6—Concept Learning - The student responds to things or events as a class; and classifying response is made to groups of ideas, things and events that appear to be dissimilar. Example: The student learns the concept *middle* by being presented with many sets of different objects arranged in a line and by generalizing that regardless of shape or size, *middle* always refers to the one between the others.

Type 5—Multiple Discrimination - Learning to discriminate among many similar-appearing stimuli and to vary the responses to verbal association as they become more numerous and complex. Example: Learning to differentiate between and among words.

Type 4—Verbal Association - The learning of chains that are verbal; learning to link combination of words as a stimuli with words as responses. Example: A student of Spanish learns that *castigo* is a word for PUNISHMENT because as she learns it and as she correctly answers a question asked by the teacher she says to herself "Another word for PUNISHMENT in English is *castigation,* so the word for *punishment* is *castigo.*

Type 3—Chaining - Learning to link a chain of two or more stimulus-response connections when they occur in rapid succession and lead to reinforcement. Example: Learning to start a car by combining the skills and observations one has already acquired.

Type 2—Stimulus-Response Learning - The acquisition of a precise response to a discriminated stimulus; voluntary actions are shaped by reinforcement. Example: A student refines the ability to pitch a "tantrum" because her movements are rewarded by having her "way" about a desired outcome.

Type 1—Signal Learning - An involuntary reflex is activated by the learning of a general, diffuse response to a signal. Since such learning involves involuntary responses, it is somewhat different from the other seven types. It is not possible to make a conclusion that Type 1 is a prerequisite for Type 2. Example: A dog salivates when the bell rings.

Grouping for Activities

To insure the involvement of all students in the desired activities, the teacher must have an in-depth knowledge of varied groupings that may be used in an instructional system. Grouping, as used in learning activities, permits students to extend previously learned concepts and principles, to make discoveries on their own, and as prescriptions for diagnosed purposes.

The Most Common Types of Grouping are:

1. Ability grouping—students with seeming similarity of ability (homogenous group);
2. Need grouping—subgrouping within ability grouping or any group who might benefit from a particular learning activity;
3. Interest grouping—subgrouping students according to their particular interests;
4. Pupil-team learning—pupil tutoring or pupils working with self-checking materials.
5. Learning centers—an environment with a set of directions for students who need additional drill or reinforcement in a given skill. They may be a phonics center, cut and paste center, library skills center, dictionary skills center, math center, reading center, spelling skills center, and writing center.
6. Interest center—unlike learning centers students use interest centers voluntarily and freely, only because they want to. The interest center generally contains games, puzzles, etc.
7. Research grouping—used with students of heterogeneous abilities to develop reports, special projects, and to collect data and information.

Selecting Learning Activities

The selection of learning activities that are relevant to specified learning objectives is a principal task for the teacher. The strategy is to select those activities most relevant to the type of instructional problem, student's characteristics, learning objectives, and subject content involved, and then make a final selection on the basis of availability, accessibility, and probable use.

A list of some active verbs that may lead to learning is given below. These verbs suggest various activities.

create	construct	invent	tell	work
visualize	experiment	act out	criticize	compute
write	collect	dramatize	judge	organize

report	exhibit	draw	evaluate	summarize
develop	display	graph	sing	analyze
interpret	visualize	paint	perform	synthesize
imagine	dance	record	exchange	travel
watch	observe	solve	research	show
demonstrate	map	chart	photograph	letter
outline	interview	edit	write	take notes
listen	read	speak	discuss	confer
speak	think			

Now, here are some examples of *activities* from the sample problem.

History

Teacher Activities:

1. Help individual students select materials.
2. Introduce topic of "Why the Revolutionary War of America" was fought.

Student Activities:

1. Reread pre-test story.
2. Participate in discussion group.

Music

Teacher Activities:

1. Circulate among students, but allow them to work by themselves.
2. Meet with each student on an individual basis before students start writing their instrumentals.

Student Activities:

1. Read the assigned chapter in textbook.
2. Review what has been discussed prior to the development of the project.

General Science

Teacher Activities:

1. Review activities and answer questions.
2. Discuss local air mass conditions for that day.

Student Activities:

1. Each student will complete the exercise in the workbook.

2. Committees to make local observations for three days about air masses and report their findings to class.

Language Arts
Teacher Activities:
1. Prepare a dramatic presentation on the history and form of rustic poetry.
2. Introduce assignment.
Student Activities:
1. Participate in rustic-poetry writing.
2. Each student will select four magazine pictures from the learning center to serve as subjects of their poems.

Mathematics
Teacher Activities:
1. Demonstrate the usages of percent and fractions.
2. Clarify any questions that students ask on subject.
Student Activities:
1. Complete the written exercise assigned.
2. Student who receives unsatisfactory scores on the written exercise will repeat any needed laboratory work. Meet again with teacher for evaluation.

Psychology
Teacher Activities:
1. Develop and discuss how the subject may be of interest to the students.
2. Conduct discussion groups.
Student Activities:
1. Sign up for discussion group.
2. Each student will criticize the relevancy of the concept *The Self-Fulfilling Prophecy.*

WORKSHEET

Develop Learning Activities:

Subject Content (or reference) _____

_____

_____

Activities:
        Teacher   *Students*

1.   1.

2.   2.

3.   3.

4.   4.

Subject Content (or reference) _____

_____

_____

Activities:
        Teacher   *Students*

1.   1.

2.   2.

3.   3.

4.   4.

Subject Content (or reference) _____

_____

_____

Activities

Teacher	Students
1.	1.
2.	2.
3.	3.
4.	4.

Subject Content (or reference) _____

_____

_____

Activities

Teacher	Students
1.	1.
2.	2.
3.	3.
4.	4.

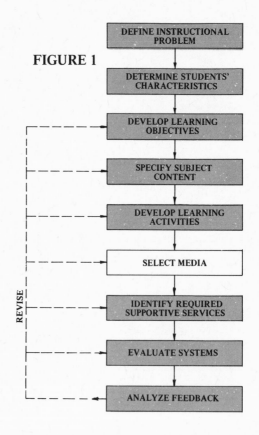

FIGURE 1

Chapter 6

Select Media

. . .What are some of the needs, problems, and opportunities involved in using certain media?

The task of selecting media is a difficult one. The taxonomy of media contains many media-stimulus characteristics. There are no clear-cut guidelines to help teachers in making the selection. Only some teachers have had a broad enough experience with the range of the taxonomy of media to have a sound basis for selecting an appropriate medium or mix of media.

Teachers need a selection model to assist them in selecting educational media that, in their judgment, most nearly meet the needs of their students. With such a model teachers are more likely to be in position to determine, systematically and more conclusively, if they are using the "best" medium or mix of media possible under a given set of constraints. The model must represent a methodology for making objective decisions for selecting appropriate media to communicate content in a desired format in terms of objectives and learning experiences. This chapter contains such a model.

Rich Experiences

A review of research has not determined "whether one medium is more effective than another in promoting learning" or "which media are best for classroom utilization?" There is little firm evidence that any medium of instruction is intrinsically or invariably superior to any other medium of instruction. Most media can readily perform most instructional functions. No single medium possesses properties which are uniquely adopted to perform one of a combination of instructional functions. A single medium will not suffice in most cases, even if only because it will become unbearably monotonous. All media perform some instructional functions well, and some not so well. Variety among media seems to be more efficient than a monopoly on one (Coger, 1972).

Media are complementary to each other and are not competitive. A combination of media in the instructional system may be superior to any one alone. As far as learning is concerned, the medium is not the message. The form of the presentation (message) influences learning too. Therefore, the *medium*, the *content* of the medium, and its *presentation form* are vital components in selecting media (Coger, 1972).

Media utilization generally promotes one or more of the following characteristics among students:

1. A quality of novelty, a fresh or new experience.
2. The involvement of one or more senses.
3. Experiences that are emotionally vivid.
4. A feeling of personal learning or achievement.
5. An awareness of the fulfillment of prior experiences,
6. The desire to learn additional subject matter or acquire new experiences.

Dale (1969) made eight general conclusions about the effectiveness of media. He said that media can do the following:

1. Heighten motivation for learning.
2. Provide freshness and variety for learning.
3. Appeal to students of varied abilities.
4. Encourage active participation of students.
5. Give needed reinforcement to students.
6. Widen the range of student experiences.
7. Assure order and continuity of thought.
8. Improve the effectiveness of other related materials.

Choosing Media for Instruction — The Selection Model

The framework for this model is focused on the contingency that planning an instructional system is a systematic process, a process containing a series of steps, no one of which is more important than the others.

The Decision Paradigm

Step 1. List the learning objectives (see chapter 3). Make sure the characterization of behavior the learner should be able to demonstrate at the end of instruction is delineated.

Step 2. Review students' characteristics (see chapter 2).

Step 3. Review specific subject content (see chapter 4).

Step 4. Review learning activities (see chapter 5).

Step 5. Identify the types of learning desired. (See chapter 5.)

Step 6. Identify the categories of the selected objectives. (See chapter 3.)

Step 7. Identify the conditions under which learning must evolve. External conditions of learning are important and are closely related to the various types of learning identified earlier.

Learning may evolve around one or more of the following learning conditions:

1. Contiguity—the most simultaneous occurrence of the stimuli and responses. Example: The teacher presents a flash card which bears the word *car*, and the children say "car."
2. Practice—the repetition of a response in the presence of the stimulus.
3. Reinforcement—one should vary the reinforcement procedures according to the desired type of learning.
4. Prerequisite previously learned.
5. Prompting and vanishing.
6. Vary order of presentation.
7. Fixed sequence.
8. Stimulate relevant recall.
9. Guide thinking.
10. Present model of performance.
11. Variety of examples.
12. Response is not stimulus bound.
13. Response generalization.
14. Teach by verbal statements.
15. Combine principles.
16. Urge new combination.
17. Employ distinctive features.
18. Discrimination.
19. Punishment.
20. The environment.

An analysis of the conditions should be made so one will be able to identify some of the limits and constraints. One must know the "ground rules" under which he or she must operate with or against.

Step 8. Select the format or presentation form of the medium or media. The selection of the specification for the media presentation form should be based on the aforementioned steps. Then pair them in the media selections process in the next step.

Tosti and Ball (1969) identified six dimensions of media presentation form. They are:

1. Encoding.
2. Duration.
3. Response demand form.
4. Response demand frequency.
5. Management form.
6. Management frequency.

Encoding dimension form is related to the ability of the media to convey data or information about the "real world." The data or information may be of four categories: (1) verbal, (2) symbolic, (3) pictorial, and (4) environmental structures.

Duration dimension is related to the length of time a given presentation remains unchanged in terms of structure. Presentation of this dimension can be in the forms of transient and persistent behaviors.

The response demand form is related to the question: "In what form will the student response be as a result of using media?" The responses may be:

1. Covert—listening, reading, observing, thinking through, meditating, imagining, etc.
2. Selective—pairing of alternatives or multiple choices.
3. Constructed—writing, drawing, typing, etc.
4. Vocal—saying something.
5. Motor—nonvocal activities not included in constructed.
6. Affective—interest, application, and emotional response.

The *response demand frequency* is conjoined with the frequency of confirmation and frequency of reinforcement in the media presentation. Programmed instruction (PI) is an example of a medium that might require such critical interaction of frequency.

The *management* form refers to the decision of how best the form can be presented. And the *management frequency* form determines the order of the presentation.

Some examples of statements one may select after considering possible presentation forms are that the presentation must:

1. Present the stimuli in a verbal or illustrated form.
2. Last no longer than the student desires it.
3. Demand a written answer from the student.
4. Be designed whereby students can respond during the presentation.
5. Demand only covert responses from students. (See Figure 2).

Step 9. This is the decision point for selecting the media-stimulus characteristics. The decision box is "is subject abstract?" requires a "yes" or "no" answer. If the subject to be presented is of the nature where it can neither be seen or heard, or experienced directly through the other senses, it is considered abstract. If the teacher answers "yes" to this decision box, he will be directed to the abstract side of the model.

The analysis of the media class here is the distinction between concrete and abstract information. Bretz (1971, pp. 32-33) listed six questions that may be used to help teachers in differentiating whether the subject is concrete or abstract. A "yes" answer to any one question means the subject is concrete and a "no" answer means the subject is abstract.

FIGURE 2

A SELECTION MODEL

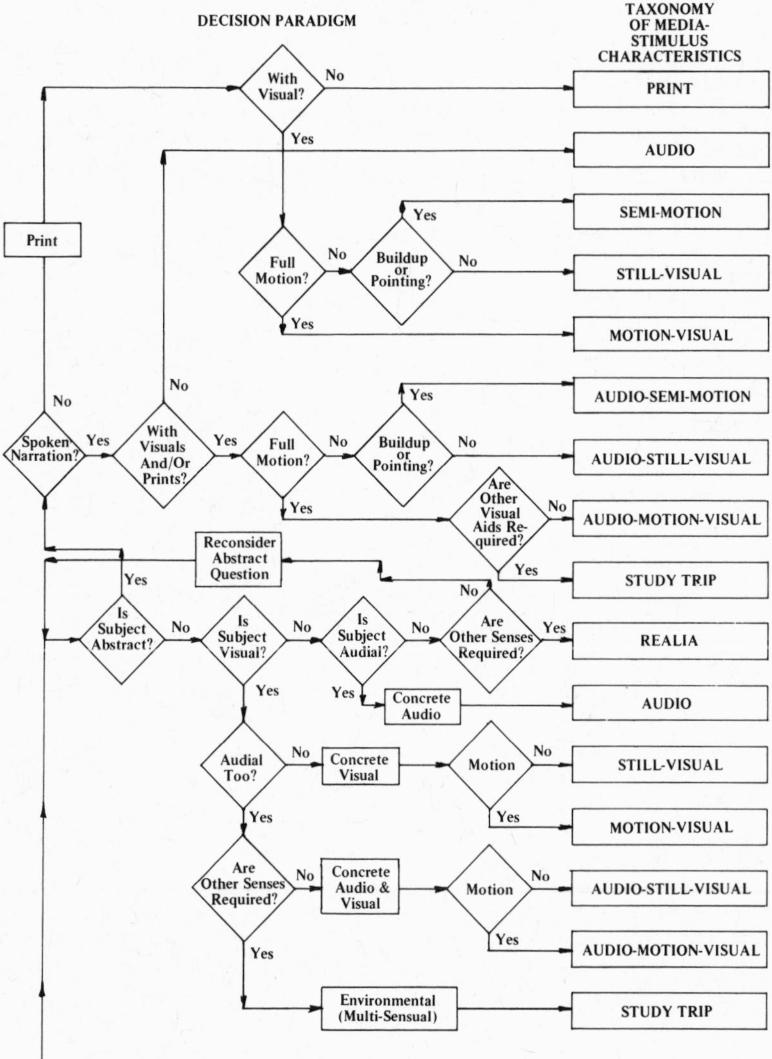

DECISION PARADIGM

TAXONOMY OF MEDIA-STIMULUS CHARACTERISTICS

INITIAL CONDITIONS (Prerequisites)

1. Identify Learning Objectives	5. Identify Types of Learning
2. Identify Students' Characteristics	6. Identify the Categories of Objectives
3. Identify Subject Contents	7. Identify the Conditions for Learning
4. Identify Learning Activities	8. Identify the Format of Medium (media)

1. Is visual recognition and identification of objects, signs, or symbols other than language symbols an objective of the lesson or required job performance?
2. Is the recognition or recall of a procedure, the physical actions or position of which are unfamiliar to the learner, one of the objectives of the lesson?
3. Is the understanding of two-dimensional physical or spatial relationships an objective?
4. Is the recall or recognition of the three-dimensional structure of some physical system or object required?
5. Is the recognition or recall of specific sounds an objective?
6. Is the appreciation of music or oral literature an objective?

For further information on the distinction between concrete and abstract information, see Edgar Dale's Cone of Experience in Chapter IV of the book, *Audiovisual Methods in Teaching.*

If the teacher has determined that the subject matter of the lesson is abstract and cannot be seen or heard, his future decision points will be located in the upper portion of the model (the abstract side).

Decision Points for Abstract Information

Briggs and Kemp identified two means of conveying abstract narration—spoken words and printed words. Bretz lists three means of narration—spoken and printed words, and pantomiming, however, he incorporated only the first two in his model. Because of its limited use, pantomiming is not included in this model.

The first decision point on the abstract side of the model is to determine if the abstract narration desired is spoken or printed. Again, Bretz (1971, p. 39) lists several questions to assist in determining whether the abstract information will be spoken or printed. If the teacher answers "yes" to any of the questions below the narration is spoken. A "no" answer means that the narration will be printed.

1. Is a substantial part of the expected learner population sufficiently unskilled in reading that audio narration would be better for them?
2. Is the personal element inherent in the spoken word important to this communication?
3. Is it important for feelings or attitudes to be conveyed?
4. Will this material be used primarily for group presentation rather than for individual purposes?
5. Is some aspect of the oral or written language arts being taught?

It should be noted here that the initial conditions (learning objectives, students' characteristics, types of learning, instructional domains, subject content, learning activities, conditions for learning, and media presentation form) delineated in the preceding steps should serve as cues in this step and the forthcoming one. Spoken words and phrases tend to be simpler; the phrases and sentences are many times shorter; fragmentary sentences often assist the listener in understanding. If the spoken words are written first, these characteristics are very unlikely to exist. However, written words can also be informal and personal. Instructional materials can be written informally and simply without detracting from the student's ability to understand.

The primary advantage of spoken narration is its effectiveness of personal and interpersonal approach in communication. Audio means are useful in conveying feelings, attitudes, and other affective objectives. Some teachers can convey emotional feelings much better through oral expression than in writing.

The primary advantage of the printed narration over audio is that print is a "non-time-based medium." There is no fixed time dimension during its presentation. Audio narrations run at a given rate, and all listeners must receive the information at that rate. Print, on the other hand, allows each reader to set his own pace. Thus when printed narration is used as an individual mode, it allows for a more efficient use of instructional time.

Print loses its advantage, however, when it is used as a group mode. Most groups have a wide range of abilities and backgrounds. One student will inevitably read faster than another—making someone bored and leaving someone else behind.

Whether to use audio and print narration in combination is an academic question that cannot be treated properly in this writing. The question is mainly one of efficiency. Does multimode narration contribute anything over the use of a single mode?

If it is decided that spoken or print narration is required, the teacher must next determine whether the spoken and written word should be used alone or with visual and/or print supports. The visual and/or print supports being discussed here are supportive aids for language communication about abstract subject matter and therefore are abstracts in themselves. When visuals are used for this purpose there is a possibility that they will distract the student. Many of the visuals are in various forms of print. Charts, graphs, diagrams and other pictorial materials are included in this category.

Visuals sometimes can make audio narration much easier to follow and easier to recall later. (Visuals as used here are considered supports and not basic materials of presentation as shown on the lower side of the model.) If a good reason for the use of visuals cannot be found, they should not be used.

The teacher should next decide if "full motion" is needed. Motion may sometimes distract from the subject. An affirmative answer to the following question should be available before one used full motion. "Is there any logical reason for using full motion visuals?"

Likewise, the decision of whether to use buildup or pointing techniques must be made by the teacher. Buildup and pointing have been classified as "semi-motion" in this writing. Buildup is defined as the building up of a subject in handwriting or drawing gradually during an instructional presentation. Items not yet discussed do not appear as visual until they are discussed. The teacher should answer the following question to help determine whether buildup is needed for his particular objective. "Is the understanding of the subject-matter concept dependent upon the sequential development of a symbolic structure?"

The other semi-motion, pointing (a pointer or spot) moves across a still-visual and calls attention to various details. The teacher should get an affirmative answer to the following question before using the semi-motion of pointing: Is the motion of pointing essential to coordinating the visual with the audio narration?

If other visuals are needed in addition to audio-motion visual, a study trip may be appropriate to consider. This class of medium and others will be discussed later.

Decision Points For Concrete Information

If a "no" answer is given at the decision-point box "is subject abstract?" and "yes" answers at "is subject visual?" and "is subject audial?" the teacher will be directed to the lower portion of the model (the concrete side). (The word "audial" was coined by Rudy Bretz to be used as a counter-part to the word "visual." "Audial," as used here, means audio, audible, capable of being heard.) Visual and audio subject-matter presentation involves the senses of seeing and hearing. Media utilization is difficult when one wants to include the other senses alone. Therefore, the question "Are other senses required?" may be found in the model. If the answer is "yes," one is directed to realia. This term will be discussed later. However, if the answer is "no" the teacher will be directed to reconsider the abstract question. This loop is included here because a teacher may consider a subject to be concrete even though it can neither be seen nor heard, nor experienced through the other senses.

If the subject is to include just an audio form of presentation the diagram points to the media class "audio." However, the subject may require a form of visual, audio-visual, or "environmental." It is considered environmental when three or more senses are required and two of the senses are seeing (visual) and hearing (audio). This category requires "real" objects either alone or in a given combination. For example: A student may be asked to go to a parking lot and count the number of cars there are or to examine a flower garden near the school for the purpose of identifying the azalea plant. Both media are environmental in structure and both allow or permit the student to use more than two of his senses. In these experiences the student can see, hear, feel, smell, or even taste if he wishes.

If the subject-matter presentation involves "audio-visual" or "visual" a decision should be made as to rather the information be presented in "motion" or in "still pictures." Probably some media are not needed in a given instructional system and could serve only to distract from the subject at hand. Bretz (1971, pp. 36-37) lists three questions that can help one in deciding if motion media are needed. A "no" answer means that still pictures are needed.

1. Is slow motion or fast motion required to portray changes that take place too rapidly or too slowly to be otherwise understandable?
2. Is the manner of movement of a subject an important characteristic for recognition of description of the subject?
3. Is the recognition or performance of a procedure, the movements of which are unfamiliar to the student, a learning objective?

The Taxonomy of Media-Stimulus Characteristics

All the decision-point boxes have been identified and discussed. As shown in the model there is a flow from these boxes to the media-stimulus characteristic boxes. The media-stimulus characteristic boxes are located at the right side of the model.

The taxonomy of media on the lower side (concrete side) of the model should be considered if media are to be the primary source of the instructional presentation. The basis for the presentation should include sensory information concerning physical characteristics, relationships, conditions, and changes in one's environment.

On the other hand, if the subject to be presented can neither be seen nor heard, nor experienced directly through any of the other senses, it is not concrete information but abstract information. The information should be described by the usage of words. The upper side (abstract side) of the model should be considered in identifying media-stimuli for meeting the initial conditions in the media presentations.

The media-stimuli on the upper side of the model was designed to assist in selecting stimuli as means to support and illustrate what is to be expressed in the code of language. It should not be used in selecting stimuli that will be used as the primary form of a presentation. The media-stimuli on the abstract portion of the model permit the student to read, hear, or see entities that bear little or no likeness to the subject matter being presented. One must deal with abstract through thoughts and general ideas. Bretz (1971) has shown that narration is one means of displaying abstract thoughts using media. Narrative words can identify, orient, locate in space and time, explain and generalize. Media-stimuli used for this purpose are referred to as "support" audio or print in this model and should be used to support and illustrate what is being expressed in language.

The taxonomy of media-stimulus characteristics are:

Realia. This form of media includes "real things, objects, specimens, samples (living or preserved, natural or man-made), and their models. Examples of realia media that may be employed in instruction are flora, artifacts, rocks, and animals.

The initial conditions may require this form of medium when two or more senses are needed for learning and the basis for selecting the media include either taste, smell, or touch. Having realia media for students to discuss, assemble, disassemble, observe, display, handle, and manipulate may be of major importance in promoting learning within the affective domain of instruction.

Realia media, like study trips, may often be the start of genuine student interest in a specific area of learning. Children in urban schools can become acquainted with a wide variety of elements located in the rural community with the utilization of realia media. Unlike study trips, realia media may be used in the local classroom.

Study trips. Sometimes called field trips, school trips, or excursions, study trips are planned visits to points outside the classroom. Organized trips of this nature may be taken to a bakery where students may not only see and hear what transpires there but also may (perhaps) taste, feel and/or smell of the environment therein. Trips may be taken within walking distance of the classroom to the school's cafeteria, maintenance shop, or the like.

Study trips permit the student to learn "in the field"; to relate what he has learned in the classroom to that of the "real world"; to relate what has been learned in the "real" world to that of the classroom.

Audio-Motion-Visual. This form of media is universal in its application. It contains all the audio, motion and visual elements. These media can be used appropriately for almost any purpose. However, these media may be less practical than some others in a selected instructional system.

Some media in this classification are: television, sound film, video tape, and picturephone. Television and picturephone permit one to see and hear "live" transmission of an event as it occurs. Television can, also, permit one to see and hear programs already recorded on film or on video tape.

The media in this classification have the potentiality for the following:

1. Create reality, reveal the invisible.
2. Offer a satisfying esthetic experience.
3. Promote an understanding of abstract relationships.
4. Compel attention.
5. Present certain meanings involving motion.
6. Heighten reality.
7. Influence and even change attitudes.
8. Speed up or slow down time.

9. Build common denominators or experiences.
10. Enlarge or reduce the actual size of objects.
11. Provide an easily reproduced record of an event.
12. Bring the distant past and the present into the classroom.

However, these same media have the potential of being expensive, to distort conclusions and impressions, and to create incoherent time and size concepts.

Audio-Still-Visual. Some of the media in this class are: sound filmstrip, sound slide-set, sound-on-slide, sound page, talking book, slow-scan television, and recorded still pictures on television. These media have most of the characteristics of audio-motion-visual media with the exception of motion.

Still visuals can show that instant moment the unaided eye cannot see. An example is the moment a bullet enters its target. Still visuals suggest time in motion but it shows, in actuality, a specific time without motion. The audio is used to complement the visual in this class of media.

Motion Visual. Silent film is the best example that can be given here to represent motion visual. It may be used to present movement: that is unfamiliar to the student; that is an important characteristic for recognition or description of a given subject; or that is required in order to portray a change in some entity.

Still Visual. Still visual may be used to enrich reading, to introduce a subject, to motivate, to translate words into symbols and to correct mistaken impressions. Some still visuals are filmstrip, model, poster, cartoon, chart, diagram, graph, map, drawing, printing, transparency, and microform.

Audio. This form of media is used when sounds, or the recognition or recall of specific sounds are an objective of the presentation of instruction. The form may also include spoken poetry, musical compositions, etc. The presentation of sound tends: to be inexpensive; to promote authenticity and realism; to foster imagination; to eliminate barriers of time and space; to promote emotionalism, to suggest immediacy and "up-to-dateness."

Audio-Semi-motion. Semi-motion with audio may be useful when full motion introduces distraction when used as an adjunct to a narration. Semi-motion permits a teacher to put a diagram, phrase, or an equation together, piece by piece, as she is talking about it. This is accomplished by using the arts of buildup and pointing. One example of semi-motion is the motion of a marker drawing a picture of a selected subject. Another is the visual growth of the line that portrays a subject.

The major advantage of semi-motion is the fact that items not yet discussed during a presentation do not appear until they are ready to be discussed and thus the viewer is less likely to be distracted by such items. Some forms of audio-semi-motion media are telewriting, audio pointer, and recorded telewriting.

Print. Print is generally regarded as a form to be used in the individual mode. It allows each reader to set his own pace. Print is intended to be read in a linear sequence, but the reader may read in any order, in any manner, and at any rate of speed the sentences and the paragraphs. Computer assisted instruction is included in this category. Prints may also be in the form of other symbols—drawing, cartoon, diagram, chart, graph, map, etc. These symbols are not used to represent the direct reality of the objects but merely to represent or symbolize them. An example of this is a rabbit foot, which represents or symbolizes *good luck.* However, it does not look like that which it stands for. Prints as abstracts however, may be rich in the meaning for which they stand.

Semi-motion. (See audio-semi-motion above.) These media-stimulus characteristics are similar to those characteristics described in audio-semi-audio characteristics.

Here are examples of *media* from our sample problems.

History

    A. Teacher Activities:

        Introduce a video tape presentation that illustrates why the American Revolutionary War was fought.

    B. Student Activities:

        View filmstrip, then complete worksheet that reviews main points.

Music

    A. Teacher Activities:

    Use overhead transparencies to show the position of notes.

    B. Student Activities:

    Use textbook to develop the four-part writing.

General Science

    A. Teacher Activities:

    Present a five-minute animated film showing types of air masses, movements, source regions, and how each is formed.

    B. Student Activities:

    Study filmstrip on air masses characteristics and weather elements.

Language Arts

    A. Teacher Activities:

    Using transparencies describe the common elements of rustic poetry.

    B. Student Activities:

    Visit a rural area for the purpose of gathering information to write a poem.

Mathematics

    A. Teacher Activities:

    Use an animated film to show the interrelatedness of percent and fraction.

    B. Student Activities:

    Follow instructions in accompanying programmed instruction booklet.

Psychology

    A. Teacher Activities:

    Show video tape on "The Concept of the Self-Fulfilling Prophecy."

    B. Student Activities:

    Develop and test the hypothesis listed at the end of the assigned chapter.

WORKSHEET

Media Needed

Media needed for teacher activities:

1.   6.

2.   7.

3.   8.

4.   9.

5.   10.

Media needed for student activities:

1.   6.

2.   7.

3.   8.

4.   9.

5.   10.

WORKSHEET

Media Need and Schedule Sheet

A. Media for large group (classroom)	Dates Needed	Ordered	Confirmed & Scheduled
1.			
2.			
3.			
4.			
5.			

B. Media for laboratory work

1.

2.

3.

4.

5.

C. Media for independent study

1.

2.

3.

4.

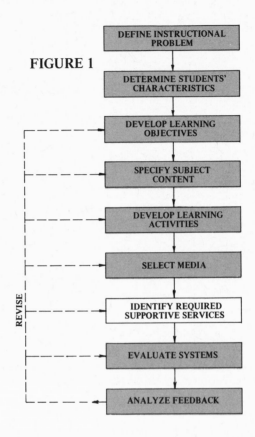

FIGURE 1

Chapter 7

Identify Required Supportive Services

. . . What support services are required to implement the instructional system?

Supportive services include personnel, time, schedules, facilities, budget, equipment (hardwares), and softwares. Frequently, teachers do not consider these necessary supportive services until they want to spend a sum of money, need a specific room, want to use a certain equipment, or require specific professional or technical assistance—this procedure should not be used in planning and using instructional systems.

It is very difficult, if not impossible, for teachers to execute most instructional systems independently. Instructional systems are seldom developed as a "one-man-show." Few of us have all the necessary skills required to develop and execute instructional systems.

Briefly, we will consider some aspects of the supportive services that may be required in most instructional systems.

Personnel

Professional assistances are sometime sought by teachers in carrying out their plans effectively. Professional skills are essential in planning and executing instructional systems. Some of the professional help a teacher may need are listed below. The teacher must realize that help may be needed to make the "system work."

1. Other teachers
2. Media specialists
3. Librarians
4. Students
5. Secretaries
6. Teacher aids and assistants
7. Technicians
8. Administrators
9. Psychometrists
10. Educational psychologists (Learning theorists)
11. Subject matter and curriculum experts
12. Instructional systems designers
13. Janitorial staff

In some instances, most teachers may feel as if they do not need any assistance and they may assume all of the roles listed above. One should be mindful that teaching should be innovative. Planning is innovative. Assistance is generally helpful when one is planning.

A key factor for success in planning an instructional system is the manner in which people work together. Decisions derived from planning should always be open to review and criticism by all members of the planning team. Some teachers may be reluctant to work in this framework because it challenges their present practices and security.

Teachers ordinarily should seek help in:

1. Selecting objectives, contents, methods, media and forms of evaluation.

2. Checking the accuracy of subject content.
3. Analyzing student progress.
4. Sequencing learning experiences.
5. Developing evaluation instruments for pre-testing, post-testing.
6. Analyzing and determining the cost effectiveness of instructional systems.
7. Arranging schedules, facilities, personnel, assignments, equipment, media, and budget allocations.
8. Preparing, installing and maintaining hardwares and softwares.
9. Locating and developing instructional materials.
10. Providing remedial or special assistance to student.
11. Administering and correcting tests.
12. Supervising laboratory and student group activities.
13. Housekeeping tasks to insure that the environment is conducive for learning.
14. Corresponding, filing, preparing reports, typing and labeling and duplicating materials.
15. Learning to operate equipment.

Schedules and Time

One of the important entities of planning is scheduling. To help insure that the system will be executed properly the activities of all participants therein must be synchronized. Proper scheduling insures smoothness of operation. Therefore, a work schedule for those participating in the system must be developed and followed.

A typical problem some teachers have is that a particular medium is available but it is not conveniently accessible. Therefore, the chosen medium is not a practical one, even though it is appropriate for a given system. This is the result of a scheduling problem.

Time must be scheduled for instructional planning. Next to personnel, the allocation of time is the most difficult element to control. Finding time for planning may be difficult. A real dedication is required to schedule one's time to include adequate planning and execution of instructional systems. The better teachers find time.

Facilities

Space needs for various activities, equipment, storage, electrical requirements and others are necessary to develop effective instructional systems. Some systems may require modifications of current space, or major or minor adaptations of additional space. Other systems might require new construction. Learn the limits and constraints of various systems before they are developed. Ideas about limits and constraints may be obtained by observing instructional systems in operation in other environments.

Facilities for instructional systems may be required to support any of the following:

1. The changing classroom environment.
2. Multi-group activities.
3. Team teaching approach.
4. Listen-response media control approach.
5. Multi-media approach.
6. Individualized instruction.
7. Small discussion-group spaces.
8. Problem-solving activities.
9. Workrooms.
10. Staff meeting rooms.
11. A resource center.

Some important questions about instructional systems relating to spaces are given below.

1. What teamwork in the classroom or laboratory shall be organized?
2. To what degree will we make courses classes for learning instead of classes for listening?
3. What kinds of research activities shall we organize?
4. What kinds of activities shall we organize to assist students in drawing conclusions and testing them?

5. How shall we help students to make valid observations?
6. How shall we provide learning experiences in which students pool and share their work?
7. When has a student learned something?
8. What conditions should be provided for students?
9. How deeply should we encourage students to probe?
10. What kinds of problems should we ask students to solve?
11. What will our students be practicing in the classroom and laboratory?

Answers to these questions point the way to decisions about changes in learning spaces. Less mistakes in designing instructional systems will be made if we turn our attention to the learners and their needs in our society.

Budget

Funds are required to develop and implement viable instructional systems. Any school system that is interested in educational excellencies must provide money for research, development and implementation. Realistically though, some school systems are interested mainly in educational survival and not educational excellency.

After carefully planned, developed and executed instructional systems have proved their worth, the results in terms of increased student learning and better use of professional services should justify the investment. Financial support may be needed for any or all of the following:

During the planning and development phases

1. Professional planning time.
2. Contractual services.
3. Construction or renovation of required facilities.
4. Purchase, installation and check-out of hardwares and softwares.
5. Purchase and preparation of educational media.
6. Development of testing and measurement devices for evaluation.

7. Cost, schedule and time for try-outs and "de-bugging."
8. Travel, postage, telephone and other administrative costs.
9. Inservice training of personnel.
10. Servicing and modifying hardwares and softwares.

During the implementation phase

1. Servicing, modifying, maintenance, and storage of hardwares and softwares.
2. Replacement of damaged, stolen, and consumable materials.
3. Salaries of personnel.
4. Contractual services.
5. Travel, postage, telephone, overhead and other administrative costs.
6. Servicing and modifying hardwares and softwares.
7. Depreciation of equipment.
8. Inservice training of personnel.
9. Costs for evaluation of systems.
10. Costs for "de-bugging" systems.

Equipment, Hardwares and Softwares

An equipment is a fixed or movable unit of furniture or furnishings, a machine, an instrument, or an apparatus that is non-expendable. Hardwares are instruments, machines and/or equipments that are used as the means of presenting the contents of softwares. Examples of hardwares are tape recorders, record players, overhead projectors, teaching machines, radios, television receivers, and motion picture projectors. Softwares are a given body of materials considered as a system of potential value when put to work by means of a hardware. Examples of some softwares (supporting materials) for the hardwares are transparencies, films, slides, film strips, programmed materials, tapes for recorders, discs for record players and radio programs (Coger, 1972).

Equipments, hardwares and softwares are necessary components of instructional systems. In some cases, they are readily available and in others they must be obtained. They generally complement each other in terms of their utilization.

The type of hardware that is available may influence the kinds of softwares to be used.

The teacher should seek professional help in selecting these items. There is such a wide variety of equipments, hardwares and softwares available today for both individual and group presentation forms that it is difficult to choose without up-to-date experiences and an extensive background. Seek help but do not leave the final decision to others.

Remember that highly sophisticated and complex hardwares are impressive and can perform many tasks. However, your system may not need these tasks performed. Often, less costly and less complex hardwares can serve equally well. Be practical and reasonable. See Appendix A.

Here are some examples of supportive services for the same problems.

History

> Budget: $100 for video tape, filmstrips, reading materials.
>
> Personnel: (1) Teacher to conduct class activities, supervise discussion group, assist each student in selecting reading materials and viewing filmstrips.
>
>   (2) Technician to operate video tape.
>
>   (3) Librarian to assist students in selecting reading materials and filmstrips.
>
> Facilities and Schedules: Regular classroom one period a day for two weeks with flexibility for rearrangement and use of filmstrip and television receiver.
>
> Equipment and Materials: Video tape recorder and three television receivers with 30-minute tape. 8 filmstrip viewers and 12 filmstrips reading materials with exercises and worksheets.

Music

> Budget: $40 for transparencies, mounted pictures and printed materials.
>
> Personnel: (1) Teacher and media specialist to plan and develop mounted pictures and transparencies.
>
>   (2) Library aide to find printed materials.

Facilities and Schedules: Regular classroom and laboratory for developing projects 50 minutes a day for one week.

Equipment and Materials: One overhead projector; textbook and other printed materials; duplicated sheets on musical notes and music sheets.

General Science

Budget: $50 for renting 16mm animated film, 60 copies of 16 frame filmstrip, textbook, workbook, and other printed materials.

Personnel: (1) Teacher to present five-minute animated film and subject content.

(2) Teacher aide to assist students in making their three-day observation, and viewing of filmstrip.

(3) Secretary to help students prepare their reports of observation.

Facilities and Schedules: Classroom for 50 minutes; small group meeting room for 5 students; 6 independent-study carrels for 4 days, 2 hours per day.

Equipment and Materials: 16mm projector, 6 filmstrip viewers; one ream of data sheets; 16mm film, 6 copies of filmstrips, textbook, workbook and other printed material.

Language Arts

Budget: $60 for preparing transparencies; study trip; other printed materials; and disc (record).

Personnel: Teacher and students are to prepare and present a dramatic presentation on the history and form of rustic poetry.

Facilities and Schedules: Learning center (will need for 50 minutes); a two-hour visit to a selected rural area; three 50 minute periods to plan drama; one class period for five days to write poems.

Equipment and Materials: Overhead projector, transparencies, printed materials, transportation, records and magazines.

Mathematics

Budget: $35 for renting film and buying programmed booklets.

Personnel: (1) Teacher to present film and explain the usages of programmed booklets.

(2) Teacher aide will assist students and teacher in answering the questions of students.

Facilities and Schedules: Regular classroom for 5-50 minute periods; students will work on an individual basis.

Equipment and Materials: 16mm projector and animated film, programmed booklets, and other printed materials.

Psychology

Budget: $15 for renting video tape.

Personnel: (1) Teacher will present content and video tape.

(2) School psychologist will discuss the concept of "self-fulfilling prophecy."

Facilities and Schedules: Regular classroom for presentation and discussion 3-45 minute periods; Psychology laboratory 2-45 minute periods.

Equipment and Materials: Television receiver and video tape, guide sheets for testing the hypothesis and sheets for observations.

WORKSHEET

Required Supportive Services

1. Personnel

2. Equipment, Hardwares & Softwares

3. Schedules and Time

WORKSHEET

Required Supportive Services

4. Facilities

5. Budget

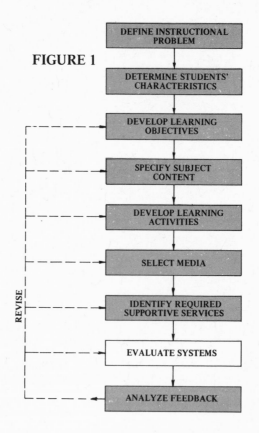

FIGURE 1

Chapter 8

Evaluation

. . . How will the amount of student learning be measured? What process will be used for delineating, obtaining, and providing useful information for decision making?

Before one makes a decision, the entities on which the decision is to be made should have been properly evaluated. Evaluation permits one to determine the degree and level of effectiveness of educational outcomes.

Stufflebeam defines evaluation as a process of delineating, obtaining and providing useful information for judging decision alternatives. It is the interpreting of data and information. It is the process of determining to what extent the objectives are actually being realized by the program or system. Since objectives are aimed to produce certain desirable changes in the behavior patterns of the students, the evaluation is used to determine the degree to which these changes in behavior are actually taking place. Evaluation is basically the identification of the degree of relationships that exist between educational inputs and educational outputs (Coger, 1972).

Within the planning sequence of designing an instructional system, the techniques for the evaluation of that system should closely follow the writing of the objectives and the defining of student characteristics. The objectives should indicate what the evaluation should be. It is highly recommended that the designing of evaluation methods, such as writing the final examination, should be developed from the given objectives.

At the present, however, most teachers design their systems of evaluation (writing final examinations) for a course, unit or topic as the teaching—time period draws to a close. The evaluation is made on the subject content covered or on what the teacher thinks the students ought to know. Little or no reference is made to objectives. One way to determine if a teacher is evaluating from a set of objectives is to review that teacher's final examination or other evaluation instruments; then compare the examination and objectives. The categories of objectives, as identified in chapter three, will be reflected in the testing.

Teacher-Evaluation Systems

Evaluation generally serves two purposes for teachers. First, it is used to determine the degree to which each student has mastered the objectives. This approach is called mastery-learning system. Secondly, evaluation is used to determine the relative standing of each student on a competitive basis such as normal-curve grading and other scaled ratings. This approach is the traditional system most teachers used.

Evaluation of the mastery learning approach is based on the usages of criterion-reference tests. Each student is judged on how well he or she attains the required level of competence and comprehension specified for each objective. In this program if all students reached or exceeded all the objectives in the system, all students get the same passing grade.

The basic assumptions and characteristics of the mastery-learning approach to evaluation is listed below:

1. Student should be assessed on an individual basis.
2. Instructional planning should be oriented toward the desired terminal behaviors.
3. Teachers should be accountable for how well students learn.
4. Instruction should focus on each learner.
5. Students have varied initial behaviors or competencies at the beginning of an instructional sequence.
6. The teacher's role is primarily that of a presenter, diagnostician, manager, and organizer.
7. Each instructional system should contain instructional strategies for individual competencies and learning styles.
8. Student achievements should be the responsibility of both the teacher and the student.
9. The performance of each student should be evaluated by comparing it with an absolute standard.
10. Formative (periodic) evaluations should be used for diagnostic purposes and should be independent of the summative (final) evaluation, the results of which is to recycle students' learning or permit them to progress.
11. Summative evaluations are for grading, such as pass-fail or satisfactory-unsatisfactory.
12. All students should achieve an established criterion level of mastery before moving to the next segment of instruction.

The implementation of a pure mastery-learning system of evaluation is sometimes impractical. Therefore, the evaluator may wish to modify it with the traditional approach. The basic assumptions and characteristics of the traditional approach to evaluation is shown below:

1. Students are assessed and grouped into four basic learning levels—A, B, C, and D.
2. Instructional Planning is oriented toward materials to be covered.
3. Teachers are not accountable for student learning.
4. Instruction is focused on the "average" student.
5. Students enter a course, unit or topic with the same level of competencies.
6. The teacher's role is primarily that of an information-dispenser.
7. Each instructional system contains instructional strategies that were selected and designed for the "average" student.
8. Student achievement is primarily the responsibility of the student.
9. Students are evaluated by comparing one student with all others in the group.
10. Periodic assessments, such as quizzes and mid-term tests, are used to determine the levels of achievement and the students are permitted to progress to the next unit of instruction regardless of the results of the assessment.
11. Periodic and/or final exams are used to determine final grade, generally some averaging procedure is used.
12. Students generally recycle or repeat the entire course if the final grade is below "C" or "D," even though some aspects of the subject were mastered.

The mastery-learning approach requires a criterion-reference system of evaluation. It should be designed to determine if a student has achieved mastery of a behavior as specified in the objective(s). Criterion-reference evaluations are used:

1. For pre-assessment purposes;
2. For formative testing (checking progress);
3. To see if a system needs modification;
4. To determine whether students achieve at given levels of competencies.

In criterion-reference systems, variabilities among students are irrelevant; results of achievements are given in binary forms: pass-fail, satisfactory-unsatisfactory; test items are constructed to measure a pre-determined level of proficiency; and the criteria for mastery are stated for usage in the evaluation. The main function is to assess whether the student has mastered a specific criterion or performance standard.

The traditional approach to evaluation is generally called norm-referenced evaluation. This form of evaluation is referred to as "norm-reference" because the learner's performance is compared with that of a normative group. This procedure promotes the concept of relative standard—one's performance is relative to how others performed on the test. A relative standard might indicate that a student answered more questions than any other student in the group, but it does not indicate whether the student answered all the questions, 70 percent of them or 30 percent of them.

In the norm-referenced systems, variabilities of scores among students are desirable; test questions are designed to discriminate among students; test results are transposed to the traditional grading system (A, B, C, D, F); and, the criterion of mastery is usually not specified. The main function of norm-referenced evaluation is to obtain a student's relative position within the normative group.

Regardless of the approach that one uses, evaluation should involve tests and instruments to measure the acquisition of knowledge, skills, and aptitudes. It is important to remember that the tests and instruments should measure the identical behavior specified in the objectives.

Below are some examples:

Cognitive Domain
Comprehension:
Objective: Given six questions presented orally in Spanish, the student will orally answer each question in English within ten minutes. Performance will be evaluated on completeness of the English responses.

Evaluation: This objective suggests an oral form of

testing. The testing procedure may involve peer evaluation, direct one-to-one interaction between the teacher and student, or a tape recording may be used.

Affective Domain
Organization:

Objective: Given a musical composition that the student selected, the student will identify the characteristics of the composition that is admired and write a composition that reflects the characteristics identified in the composition that was selected. The composition should be developed within five days.

Evaluation: The mode of evaluation is the writing of the composition and the specificities of the characteristics in the composition. The other students in the class and the teacher can provide feedback on how clearly the given characteristics are reflected in the composition developed.

Psychomotor Domain
Complex Overt Response:

Objective: Given an untuned motor from a Pinto car and three hours, the student will replace the necessary parts and make the necessary adjustments so it operates at maximum capacity.

Evaluation: This behavior should be assessed in the same manner a tune-up shop will assess the performance of the motor. Testing of this sort provides students with practice and also affords the opportunity for the teacher to give immediate feedback.

Pre-assessment

Before changes in behavior can be measured adequately it is desirable to assess students entering behaviors. See Chapter 2. The pre-test should determine (1) how much of the topic, unit, or course the students already know prior to the instruction; (2) whether the students have the necessary behavior capabilities for the proposed instruction; and (3) what instructional activities should be prescribed for each student.

The pre-test or pre-assessment should be based on specific learning objectives designated for the unit. The results of the pre-test may indicate (1) whether the student may omit any of the objectives in the unit; (2) whether any student will need to master prerequisite skills before beginning the unit; and (3) what specific instructional activities should be provided for each student. The above recommendations imply individualized instruction. It is, however, possible to require prerequisite behavioral competencies and omit objectives for individual students in group-pace instruction.

The results of the pre-assessment may mandate changes in objectives and instructional procedures whereby, ideally, all students achieve all required objectives. Modifications may be necessary in the instructional system, also, on the basis of changing values, new research findings, observed results and new developments and techniques.

The most important factors one should remember about the form of evaluation are these:

1. The results of evaluation must be used for informing students and other interested persons about the degree of success of each student in a given topic, unit or course.
2. It is the success of the instructional system, as well as those of the students that is being evaluated.
3. Unsuccessful instructional systems is probably the result of one of the following:
   a. The measurement process may have been inadequate.
   b. The students were motivated inadequately before or during the instruction.
   c. The objectives were too difficult for students.
   d. The students did not have the prerequisites necessary to enter the instructional system.
   e. The instructional activities were designed inadequately.
   f. The students were provided insufficient time to master the objectives.
   g. The objectives were unrealistic.

Evaluating the Effectiveness of Instructional Systems

This section contains an effectiveness model which was designed to assist teachers in evaluating the effectiveness of instructional systems. This model permits teachers to select and use the most appropriate and practical instructional systems. It treats specific applications of local conditions in its design.

A system may be appropriate for a given need and may or may not be practicable as well. To be considered appropriate a system needs only to be capable of expressing the desired message. Practicability of systems involves the consideration of local conditions, such as availability, accessibility, acceptability, reliability, validity and cost. For example, a 16mm color film would be appropriate for systems in which the initial conditions involve visual recognition; however, it might be too costly for utilization in a low-enrollment course.

The interpretation of the measure of effectiveness is the desired percentage of students reaching an acceptable level of achievement for each objective. This information should be a matter of record that can easily be presented in a table or chart. This means that the teacher should determine how many students accomplished the stated objectives within the time set.

As you proceed to evaluate a system keep in mind that the planning sequence for evaluation should closely follow the writing of the objectives. The objectives should indicate what the evaluation should be.

The Steps in Using the Effectiveness Model

The model contains four sections—(1) selection process (2) appropriateness process, (3) practicability process, and (4) evaluation process.

The selection process includes steps 1 through 3. It provides a system whereby one can select alternative instructional systems. The appropriateness process includes steps 4 through 8. Steps 9 through 11 are components of the practicability process. The evaluation process includes steps 12 through 15. See Figure 3.

A General Account of the Procedure

Step 1. Make a decision on which instructional systems will solve the instructional problem. More than one system or combination of systems should be selected. This will permit you to use all but one of the selected systems as alternatives in solving the instructional problem. The main prerequisites to step 1 are the pre-assessment of learners and the adjustment of objectives. Choosing the mode(s) of instruction is important in this step. See Appendix B.

Step 2 Identify all of the recognizable potentials each selected instructional system has in relation to the given instructional problem. This delineating process will be useful in determining if the selected alternatives can be adopted in the desired instructional environment. In the delineating process some typical questions that should be asked are listed below.

Will the instruction:

1. Appeal to learners of varied abilities?
2. Encourage active participation of all students?
3. Provide for reinforcement of learning?
4. Promote freshness and variety in its format?
5. Advance the concept of motivation for learning?
6. Extend the range of the experiences of learners?
7. Assure order and continuity of thought in solving the instructional problem?

The potentialities of instructional systems cannot be adequately discussed here. It is a process of identifying and delineating information required through an inventory of decision alternatives.

Step 3. The task in this step is to make a tentative decision about the most appropriate instructional system(s) from the selected alternatives identified in step 1. The decision should be based on information gathered in step 2. Before this process becomes operational two things must be known: (1)

FIGURE 3

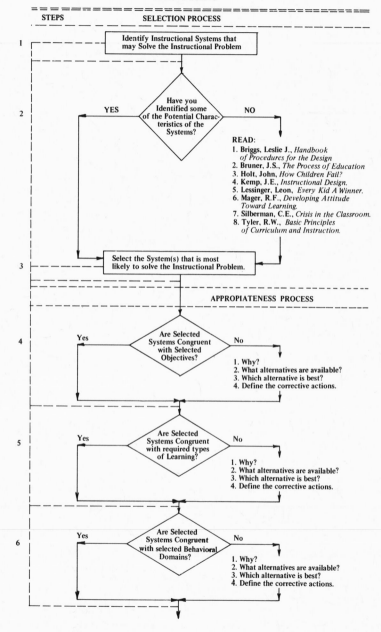

STEPS   SELECTION PROCESS

1

Identify Instructional Systems that
may Solve the Instructional Problem

2

YES   Have you
Identified some
of the Potential Charac-   NO
teristics of the
Systems?

READ:
1. Briggs, Leslie J., *Handbook
   of Procedures for the Design*
2. Bruner, J.S., *The Process of Education*
3. Holt, John, *How Children Fail?*
4. Kemp, J.E., *Instructional Design.*
5. Lessinger, Leon, *Every Kid A Winner.*
6. Mager, R.F., *Developing Attitude
   Toward Learning.*
7. Silberman, C.E., *Crisis in the Classroom.*
8. Tyler, R.W., *Basic Principles
   of Curriculum and Instruction.*

3

Select the System(s) that is most
likely to solve the Instructional Problem.

APPROPIATENESS PROCESS

4

Yes   Are Selected
Systems Congruent
with Selected   No
Objectives?

1. Why?
2. What alternatives are available?
3. Which alternative is best?
4. Define the corrective actions.

5

Yes   Are Selected
Systems Congruent
with required types   No
of Learning?

1. Why?
2. What alternatives are available?
3. Which alternative is best?
4. Define the corrective actions.

6

Yes   Are Selected
Systems Congruent
with selected Behavioral   No
Domains?

1. Why?
2. What alternatives are available?
3. Which alternative is best?
4. Define the corrective actions.

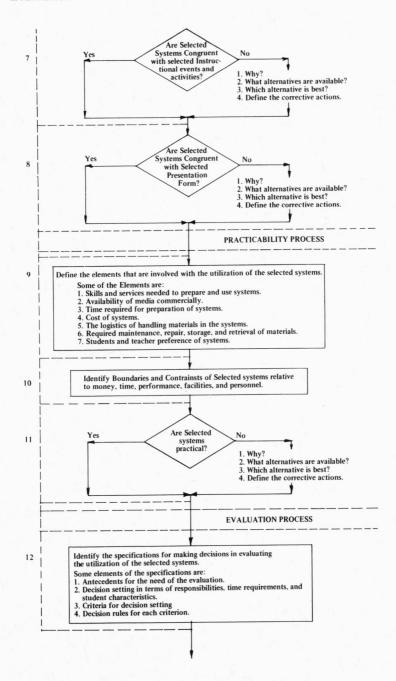

7
Are Selected Systems Congruent with selected Instructional events and activities?
Yes
No
1. Why?
2. What alternatives are available?
3. Which alternative is best?
4. Define the corrective actions.

8
Are Selected Systems Congruent with Selected Presentation Form?
Yes
No
1. Why?
2. What alternatives are available?
3. Which alternative is best?
4. Define the corrective actions.

PRACTICABILITY PROCESS

9
Define the elements that are involved with the utilization of the selected systems.

Some of the Elements are:
1. Skills and services needed to prepare and use systems.
2. Availability of media commercially.
3. Time required for preparation of systems.
4. Cost of systems.
5. The logistics of handling materials in the systems.
6. Required maintenance, repair, storage, and retrieval of materials.
7. Students and teacher preference of systems.

10
Identify Boundaries and Contrainsts of Selected systems relative to money, time, performance, facilities, and personnel.

11
Are Selected systems practical?
Yes
No
1. Why?
2. What alternatives are available?
3. Which alternative is best?
4. Define the corrective actions.

EVALUATION PROCESS

12
Identify the specifications for making decisions in evaluating the utilization of the selected systems.

Some elements of the specifications are:
1. Antecedents for the need of the evaluation.
2. Decision setting in terms of responsibilities, time requirements, and student characteristics.
3. Criteria for decision setting
4. Decision rules for each criterion.

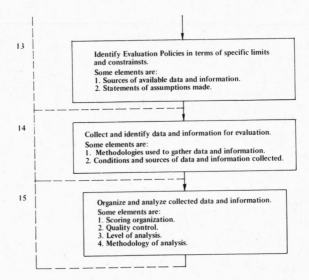

13

Identify Evaluation Policies in terms of specific limits and constrainsts.

Some elements are:
1. Sources of available data and information.
2. Statements of assumptions made.

14

Collect and identify data and information for evaluation.

Some elements are:
1. Methodologies used to gather data and information.
2. Conditions and sources of data and information collected.

15

Organize and analyze collected data and information.

Some elements are:
1. Scoring organization.
2. Quality control.
3. Level of analysis.
4. Methodology of analysis.

what alternative system(s) are to be considered and (2) what standards will be applied in choosing among the alternatives?

This is a complex decision which cannot be done as easily as it might appear. The tentative required system(s) must be selected for optimum utilizations. This demands a process of judging based on available information of the alternative systems.

Step 4. This is a process to determine if the selected instructional system and the proposed contents therein are congruent with the actual conditions of the objectives selected. This will help to diagnose any problems that might prevent required needs from being met. It will provide one of the bases for quality control or monitoring the utilization of the system(s).

This step seeks conformance. It is referred to as context evaluation. The purpose of context evaluation is to define the relevant environment and describe the desired and actual conditions pertaining to that environment.

If a discrepancy exists among the selected system(s), the subject contents, and the learning objectives, one should (1) determine why the discrepancy exists, (2) seek out alternative solutions, (3) select the alternative that is considered to be most appropriate and (4) define the corrective actions. Every question at this step implies a criterion, new information and a decision.

Step 5. This step, like step 4, is a monitoring process. It requires context evaluation. The task is to determine if the selected system(s) and subject contents are congruent with the required types of learning desired. If a discrepancy exists, it should be eliminated. The types of learning desired should have been selected as part of the initial conditions. The eight different types of learning were identified and discussed in Chapter 5.

Step 6. This is a monitoring process, like the earlier two steps. The task is to determine if the taxonomies of the behavior domains shown in the selected system(s) are congruent with the taxonomies of behavior domains specified in the initial conditions. The question to be answered here is whether the selected system(s) and subject contents are designed to promote and develop the desired (1) knowledge and information, (2) attitudes and appreciation and/or (3) skills and performances.

Step 7. This step, too, is a monitoring process. The task is to determine if the instructional events and activities, and their contents are congruent with the specifications asked for in the initial conditions.

Step 8. The significant feature of this step is that it requires one to determine if the selected system(s) and contents are congruent with the presentation form specified in the initial conditions. The variable, presentation form, can influence learning. It is an entity that is not considered often in designing instructional systems.

Step 9. Is the proposed instructional system practical? What are the elements (budget, facilities, personnel, equipment, hardwares, softwares, schedules and time) involved?

This step, like steps 10 and 11, is designed to determine the practicability of selected system(s). Practicability involves many elements. Among these are cost relative to those of other equally appropriate alternatives, acceptability to learners and teachers, availability and accessibility, skills and services needed to prepare and use, the logistics of utilization, interchangeability of softwares and hardwares, and the required maintenance, repair, storage and retrieval of systems. See Chapter 7.

To determine the practicability of a system one must know the local conditions and the specific applications of the system. This information will serve as a data base to determine the practicability of systems as well as the effectiveness of those same systems. Determining the effectiveness of systems is a sequence to the determination of the practicability of systems.

Step 10. Identify boundaries, constraints and limitations of using the selected systems. This step requires you to consider the limitation as compared to the advantages, and to consider ways of overcoming these limitations. Each system has its built-in limitations relative to cost, cost-effectiveness, comparative-benefit, trade-off, time to develop, supportive services required, scheduling, facilities and equipment needed, and others. The needs for using a given system should be determined by many of the above factors.

Step 11. This step is designed to determine if the selected system is practical for classroom utilization. Information gathered at this point should be used to determine if the local conditions and applications of instruction can be treated by the system selected.

Practicability involves:

1. Availability and accessibility.
2. Cost—comparative cost, cost—effectiveness, and trade-offs.
3. Reliability and validity.
4. Special training required for effective usage.
5. Interchangeability of softwares and/or hardwares.
6. Acceptability to learners and teachers.
7. Supportive services required.
8. Others.

Step 12. This step requires a "yes" or "no" answer. Move to the next step only if the answer is "yes."

It is assumed that before entering this step the decision has been made to evaluate the utilization of the system. This is the first of four steps in evaluating the instructional systems. It is essential that the boundaries elements and their characteristics be defined and delimited to a manageable proportion before the evaluation process begins. Some methods and sources that might be useful in this process include: reviewing information gathered in steps 1 to 11 in this model, needs assessment, system analysis, network-based management tools, and methods-means selection processes. These methods and sources will provide the necessary information to define and delimit the entire evaluation process to a manageable size.

After the above process has been completed, write the specifications to be used in evaluating the effects of the utilization of the system.

The proposed procedure is:

1. *Identify and explicate the need for the evaluation.* List the antecedents which make the evaluation necessary.

2. *Determine the decision setting.* What types of decisions will be made? (1) planning decisions to determine objectives; (2) structuring decisions to design procedures; (3) implementing decisions to utilize, control and refine procedures; and/or (4) recycling decisions to judge and react to attainments. What is the decision setting? (1) Homeostasis (a small degree of change is desired as determined by the use of a high level of information grasp); (2) incrementalism (a small degree of change is desired and a low level of information grasp); (3) metamorphism (large degree of change is desired and high level of information grasp); (4) neomobilism (large degree of change is desired and a low level of information grasp).

   The role here is to determine the types of decisions to be made and the decision setting in which the data and information collected are to be used. This step permits you as a decision maker to determine what kinds of decisions must be made and, as an evaluator, to determine what data and information are needed in order to make the required kinds of decisions.

   Some sub-steps may include the time for the decision setting, the responsibilities required for making the decision, and the influence the decision will have on others.

3. *Identify the criteria for decision setting.* The criteria contain the standards that will be used in making the decisions about the worth of the system used. The rules for the decision setting may consist of a number of criterion variables. Each variable should contain a number of questions to be answered. Each proposed question should produce at least two alternative answers. Each alternative answer will have some implications for alternative actions.

4. *Identify the decision rules.* A decision rule must be set for each criterion variable to be evaluated. The variables to be measured are the operationalization of the questions to be answered. There are three distinct kinds of decisions. *Action decision* involves selecting from two or more alternatives available. *Qualitative decision* involves the determination of the worth or the state (effectiveness) of a system. *Quantitative decision* involves time, numbers, or other measures of quantity.

Step 13. In this step you should identify the degree of freedom and constraints under which you will work to collect the data and information. This is one means of determining the evaluation policies that will be included in the process of evaluation.

This Process may entail:

1. Specifying the sources of information that will be available whereby the process of evaluation can take place.
2. Explicating all the tasks involved in the proposed evaluation.
3. Identifying the limitations involved in the above.
4. Selecting evaluation assumption. The assumption should be related to questions you wish to have answered as a result of the evaluation.

The major question to ask here is "what activities will I accept as evidence of the achievement wanted?" The specifications that will aid in answering this question should be stated so that:

1. The conditions under which the systems are expected to perform are known.
2. The essential characteristics of the desired outcomes are known.
3. The phraseology of the specifications should be written in the form of expectations.
4. The expected outcomes are described so that they can be observed by others.

5. The expectations should be reasonable and attainable.
6. The criteria should be specified so that they can be measured.

This is the last step that can be completed without having to use the instructional system. The post-utilization steps will follow.

Step 14. The obtaining of data and information is vital in this step. The procedure for the collection of data and information includes:

1. The listing of data and information and their sources;
2. The methodology and instrument used in the collection process;
3. The conditions under which the data and information were collected.

Step 15. The providing of data and information is vital in this step. The collected data and information must be organized, analyzed, identified and clarified. The magnitude of this task is dependent mainly upon the level of decisions to be made, the information needed to make those decisions, and the organization of data gathered.

This process should include the following tasks:

1. Identify the kinds of information you have or think you have as a result of the evaluation.
2. Identify other kinds of information that might be needed before you can proceed to make some decisions about the evaluation.
3. Who are some other people that may become involved in making decisions about the evaluation?
4. Are there any conflicts of interest involved in this evaluation?
5. To what extent if any is there a time variable to be considered in terms of the situation before you.

Because evaluation is multi-faceted, no samples (examples) of evaluation will be listed in this chapter.

WORKSHEET

Evaluation of Instructional System

Step 1: _____ Step 9: _____

Step 2: _____ Step 10: _____

Step 3: _____ Step 11: _____

Step 4: _____ Step 12: _____

Step 5: _____ Step 13: _____

Step 6: _____ Step 14: _____

Step 7: _____ Step 15: _____

Step 8: _____

WORKSHEET

Student Mastery Test
Cognitive Domain

Test Number_____

Concepts and objectives to be tested
       (Unit or Module Reference Numbers) _____

Items: (Include Correct Answers to Objective Items)

   1. Unit or Module number, objective number, and cognitive
                            level. (   )
     Item:

   2. Unit or Module number, objective number, and cognitive
                            level. (   )
     Item:

   3. Unit or Module number, objective number, and cognitive
                            level. (   )
     Item:

   4. Unit or Module number, objective number, and cognitive
                            level. (   )
     Item:

   5. Unit or Module number, objective number, and cognitive
                            level. (   )
     Item:

   6. Unit or Module number, objective number, and cognitive
                            level. (   )
     Item:

WORKSHEET

Student Mastery Test
Psychomotive Domain

Test Number _____

Concepts and objective to be tested
(Unit or Module Reference Numbers) _____

Items: (Include Correct Answers to Objective Items)

1. Unit or Module number, objective number, and psychomotive level. (   )
   Item:

2. Unit or Module number, objective number, and psychomotive level. (   )
   Item:

3. Unit or Module number, objective number, and psychomotive level. (   )
   Item:

4. Unit or Module number, objective number, and psychomotive level. (   )
   Item:

5. Unit or Module number, objective number, and psychomotive level. (   )
   Item:

6. Unit or Module number, objective number, and psychomotive level. (   )
   Item:

WORKSHEET

Student Mastery Test
Affective Domain

Test Number _____

Concepts and objectives to be tested
(Unit or Module Reference Numbers) _____

Items: (Include Correct Answers to Objective Items)

1. Unit or Module number, objective number, and affective
level. (   )
Item:

2. Unit or Module number, objective number, and affective
level. (   )
Item:

3. Unit or Module number, objective number, and affective
level. (   )
Item:

4. Unit or Module number, objective number, and affective
level. (   )
Item:

5. Unit or Module number, objective number, and affective
level. (   )
Item:

6. Unit or Module number, objective number, and affective
level. (   )
Item:

WORKSHEET

Evaluation Summary

Unit or Module Number _____

Objective Test Analysis:

A.   Items   Number Correct   Number Incorrect

    1.

    2.

    3.

    4.

    5.

    6.

    7.

    8.

B.   Grading Procedure Used:

C.   Grade Distribution Report:
    Passed   Failed   A   B   C   D   F   Others
Number:

Percentage:

D.   Comments:

WORKSHEET

Evaluation Summary

Unit or Module Number _____

Subjective Test Analysis:

A.   Items Analysis Commentary:

      1.

      2.

      3.

      4.

      5.

B.   Grading Procedure Used:

C.   Grade Distribution Report:

Passed	*Failed*	*A*	*B*	*C*	*D*	*F*	*Others*

Number:

Percentage:

D.   Comments:

WORKSHEET

Evaluation Summary

Unit or Module Number _____

Additional Inventory Analysis:

A.   Item Analysis (Frequency of Response):

  1.

  2.

  3.

  4.

  5.

  6.

B.   Survey Analysis:

C.   Comments:

WORKSHEET

Evaluation Summary

Unit or Module Number _____

Additional Inventory Analysis:

A.   Item Analysis (Frequency of Response):

     1.

     2.

     3.

     4.

     5.

     6.

B.   Survey Analysis:

C.   Comments:

WORKSHEET

Evaluation Summary

Unit or Module Number _____

Additional Inventory Analysis:

A.   Item Analysis (Frequency of Response):

     1.

     2.

     3.

     4.

     5.

     6.

B.   Survey Analysis:

C.   Comments:

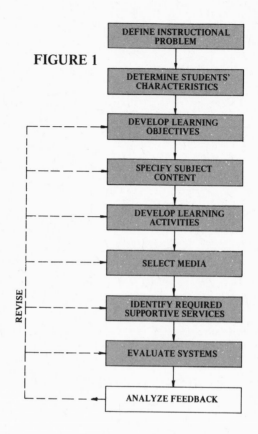

FIGURE 1

Chapter 9

Analyze Feedback

... Using the results from the evaluation, what decisions are you able to make?
... How would you revise the instructional system if you were to re-run it?

This chapter deals with the idea of making professional judgment about the results of instructional systems. The judgments or decisions should be made about the effectiveness of systems used.

Knowledge of results is commonly called *feedback*. Feedback can serve as a motivating force to regulate the instructional system. It can influence one's behavior primarily by the incongruity between the output from a set of circumstances and some standards within the system. This incongruity, or dissonance, may be a discrepancy between "what is" and "what ought to be."

Therefore, the elements which provide information concerning the results or effectiveness of the instructional system is feedback. It is a process which involves the teacher in making a decision concerning her practices. She may decide to change or revise the objectives, media, methods, and/or subject content.

Students appreciate feedback, too. Effectiveness and efficiency are increased when the students are kept informed concerning their progress.

Two factors should have been evaluated at this point: the students and the systems. Now a decision or judgment must be made relative to the information gathered through the evaluative process. This information (feedback) should serve as the bases for "changing the system," "keeping the system," or "producing more within the same system."

Evaluation is not a terminal activity. It is the bases from which decisions are made. While it is assumed here that two or more states of affair are available to select from, it is worth the time to make sure that a "real" choice or decision is open to the teacher. If there is no "real" choice or decision, then the decision-making process tends to take care of itself.

Based on information developed in the evaluation process, decision settings and decision rules should be such that one can make a decision on the systems used. The particulars to the type of decision desired should be delineated.

The actual making of the decision may involve many steps for the teacher. Before the decision can be made, maybe, much of the information gathered must be reviewed in detail or additional information may be required.

The decision to be made may be of the nature that an immediate feedback of the consequences of making that decision will be available. Decisions of this nature are related to the proximity of the consequence produced by the decisions and to the notion of immediacy. Likewise, a decision may have grown out of an immediate situation like the above but is related to some future-time orientation. This form of decision is related to the accomplishment of long range goals for which there is no immediate indication of the consequences produced from making the decision. It too will have very little, if any, indication of the extent to which the decision may have contributed to the attainment of the long-range goal. In making a decision of this nature a teacher need not be concerned with making himself vulnerable. Because the proximity of consequences is so far removed from the immediate situation, the teacher can reach a decision with either reduced or nonexistent consideration of self as a major variable in need of protection.

Some decisions may be double edged. A teacher may wish to create a climate of immediate feedback as well as work toward a long-range goal simultaneously. There is nothing unusual or unacceptable about making such decisions. What is important, however, is that the teacher be aware consciously of the kinds of decisions he must make before he attempts to make the decisions.

The decision should be made from the data and information gathered in the evaluation. However, other circumstantial variables may demand a decision before sufficient (or obtainable) data and information can be obtained. In such a case, the teacher should attempt to identify the kinds of information she does have, and make the best decisions she can. Decisions relating to artistic behaviors are generally made in this manner.

If sufficient data and information are available, the teacher must make certain decisions. The decision may be that additional information is needed or that a decision will not be made at this time. Howbeit, the decision can be of two basic types: an interpretation given to gathered information; and the generalization derived from the specific data available to the decision maker (the teacher) in treating the information. These types of decisions should be made with reference to the three kinds of decisions explained earlier and with the decision settings and the decision rules.

If the decision involves interpretation it should be of such that it embraces the ordering and reordering of items of information in such a way that one can make use of the information explained and described and use it in guiding her in additional thinking in a particular area. The information is given its meaning by the decision maker viewing it. Through this process one is saying that "it seems to me" that this is the result. It is the decision maker's duty to make sense out of available information by putting that information into some meaningful context to see what sort of patterns or relationships between the information and context emerge.

If the decision is made by some form of generalization, it may involve a principle or hypothesis induced or derived from a set of particulars developed in the initial condition in the selection model. Unlike interpretation, generalization represents a conclusion with potential relevance to a large population that may include a number of items that are not otherwise similar in any respect. One may use generalizations to predict unknown outcomes based on observable outcomes. See Figure 4.

In determining the effectiveness of instructional systems, it seems difficult, if not impossible, to develop a set of pure generalizations. Some degree of subjectivity may enter the process. However, either of the two types of decisions may be needed in making viable decisions.

FIGURE 4

THE PROCESS OF DECISION MAKING

1. Identify the decision situation.
2. Identify unmet needs and unsolved problems.
3. Identify opportunities which could be used.
4. State the decision situation in question form.
5. Specify authority and responsibility for making decisions.
6. Formulate decision alternatives.
7. Specify criteria which will be employed in assessing alternatives.
8. Determine decision rules for use in selecting an alternative.
9. Estimate the timing of the decision.

10. Obtain and assess criterion information related to each decision alternative.
11. Apply the decision rules.
12. Reflect on the efficiency of the indicated choice.
13. Confirm the indicated choice, or reject it and recycle.
14. Fix responsibility for implementing the chosen alternative.
15. Operationalize the selected alternative.
16. Reflect on the face validity of the operationalized alternative.
17. Execute the operationalized alternative, or recycle.

Teachers must take into consideration the possible implications of the decisions they will make or have made. They should consider the effects the decision will have on instruction. This will encourage teachers to articulate the observed outcomes and the decisions made.

This is a post-facto consideration as to whether the instructional systems selected and used were effective. The question here is "What is the state or prevailing condition that was created by using System X?" "How accountable are the media, methods and contents that were used?" "Did the systems do what they were purported or expected to do?"

In this process one should make an analysis of the resources and efforts invested into the system and determine how they relate to results achieved. This is a step of simply assessing the performance of the system with other conditions in the environment. This assessment can best be performed by reviewing the results of actions taken in the entire system. This process rests on the general principle that each participant in an educational process should know what educational outcomes he has affected by his actions and decisions.

WORKSHEET

Making Decisions

Based on the evaluation of the unit, topic, or course called:

_____

1. I will repeat this instructional system as designed.

2. I will revise and repeat this instructional system with the intent of strengthening it in the following ways:

    1.

    2.

    3.

    4.

    Etc.

3. I have decided not to repeat this instructional system for the following reasons:

    1.

    2.

    3.

    4.

    Etc.

4. I will develop a new instructional system to replace the current one for the following reasons:

    1.

    2.

    3.

    4.

Instructor's Name: _____ Date:_____

Appendix A

Taxonomy of Media-Stimulus Characteristics

Class 1: *Audio-Motion-Visuals*
Television, sound film, video tape, holographic recording and picturephone.

Class 2: *Audio-Still-Visual*
Sound pages, talking books, sound-on-slide, sound-slide set, sound filmstrip, recorded-still telephone, time-shared television, and slow-scan television.

Class 3: *Audio-Semi-Motion*
Telewriting and audio Pointers.

Class 4: *Motion-Visuals*
Silent films.

Class 5: *Still-Visuals*
Printed pages, filmstrip, picture set, microforms, video files, transparencies, holography, cartoons, comics, posters, charts, diagrams, maps, and globes.

Class 6: *Semi-Motion*
Telautograph.

Class 7: *Audio*
Telephone, radio, audio disc and audio tape.

Class 8: *Print*
Computers, printed pages, teletypes and punched tape.

Class 9: *Study Trip*
Museums, parks, farms, and other community resources.

Class 10: *Realia*
Mock-ups, cut-aways, kits, specimens, objects, models, dioramas, laboratories, simulations, and games.

Appendix B

Some Instructional Modes

1. Lecture

2. Independent Research.

3. Student — Student Discussions.

4. Student — Faculty Discussions.

5. Laboratory Work.

6. Field Experiences.

7. Senior Leadership Programs.

8. Independent Study.

9. Seminars.

10. Gaming and Simulation.

11. Programmed Instructions.

12. Computer Assisted Instructions.

13. Selective Text Readings.

14. Recitations.

15. Tutorial Programs.

16. Demonstration.

17. Viewing Television, 16mm Films, Filmstrips, etc.

Appendix C

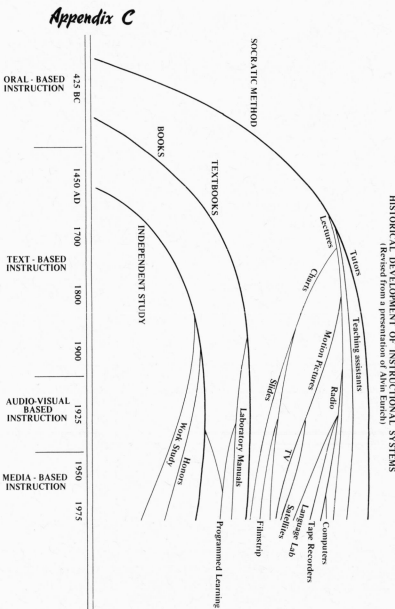

HISTORICAL DEVELOPMENT OF INSTRUCTIONAL SYSTEMS
(Revised from a presentation of Alvin Eurich)

ORAL - BASED INSTRUCTION

TEXT - BASED INSTRUCTION

AUDIO-VISUAL BASED INSTRUCTION

MEDIA - BASED INSTRUCTION

425 BC · 1450 AD · 1700 · 1800 · 1900 · 1925 · 1950 · 1975

SOCRATIC METHOD

BOOKS

TEXTBOOKS

INDEPENDENT STUDY

Lectures

Tutors

Charts

Teaching assistants

Motion Pictures

Radio

Slides

TV

Language Lab

Satellites

Tape Recorders

Computers

Laboratory Manuals

Work Study

Honors

Filmstrip

Programmed Learning

Appendix D

BALANCING THE BEHAVIOR TAXONOMIES

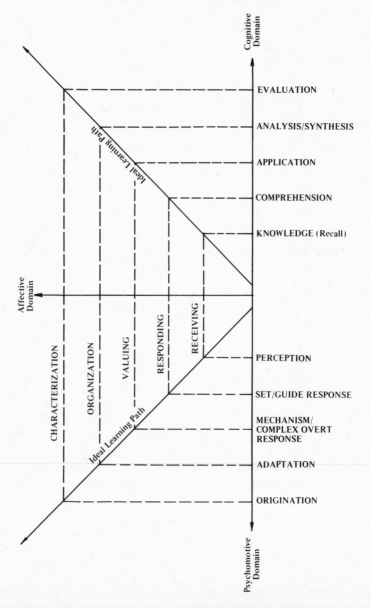

Appendix E

A Decision Paradigm

I. Definition of the Instructional System — Delimit the system to a manageable proportion.

II. Specifications — to Decisions.
    A. Describe antecedents — what events, pressure and information led to the need for the evaluation.
    B. Statement of decision setting — who has the responsibilities for various decisions?
    C. Criterion Variables — the operationalization of the questions to be answered.
    D. Decision Rules — what rules will you follow in making decisions?
    E. Available Evidence — what data and information are available?

III. Evaluation Policies.
    A. Access to Data Sources — sources of information available.
    B. Access to Data Base — the policy for data utilization.
    C. Evaluation of Authority's Role — "who does what?"
    D. Role of Evaluation Responsibility — "who is responsible for what?"
    E. Budgetary Limitations — funds available.
    F. Scheduling Limitations — by what date must the evaluation be made?
    G. Reporting Policies — rules for reporting information.

IV. Evaluation Assumptions for Sampling, Treatment of Information, Testing and Measurement and Analysis.

V. Obtaining Information.
    A. Collection of Data — sources instrumentation.
    B. Organization of Data — procedure and methodologies.
    C. Analysis of Data — sources and methodologies.

VI. Make and Report Decisions.

Appendix J

Sources For Instructional Objectives

For teachers who do not wish to write their own instructional objectives, the list below was developed.

Objectives	*Sources*
Objectives for all subject areas. . . .	The CO-OP Center for Educational Research University of Massachusetts Amherst, Massachusetts 01002
	Mr. John A. Stefani Project Spoke 37 West Main Street Norton, Massachusetts 02766
	Directory of Sources of Measurement Objectives Dr. John Ahlenius, Consultant Assessment and Evaluation State Office Building Denver, Colorado 80203
	Instructional Objectives Exchange Post Office Box 24095 Los Angeles, California 90024
	Fort Lincoln New Town Objective General Learning Corporation 5454 Wisconsin Avenue, N.W. Washington, D.C.

UNIPAC Objectives
Institute for the Development of
    Ed. Advancement (IDEA)
University of California
Suite 950
1100 Glendon Avenue
Los Angeles, California 90024

Objectives for Reading,
    Math and Science. . . .

IPI Objectives
Dr. Robert Scanlon
1700 Market Street
Philadelphia, Pennsylvania 19103

LRA Objectives
Learning Research Associates
1501 Broadway
New York, New York 10036

Objectives for Math. . . .

Clark County Objectives
Clark County School District
2832 East Flamingo Road
Las Vegas, Nevada 89109

Individualized Mathematics Sys-
    tems Objectives (IMS)
Mr. Edwar Bruchak
Regional Education Lab for the
    Carolinas and Virginia
613 Vickers
Durham, North Carolina 27701

PRIMES OBJECTIVES
Doris Cresswell
Educational Research Associates
Bureau of General and Academic
    Education
Department of Education
Box 911
Harrisburg, Pennsylvania 17125

Objectives for Metric
    Education. . . .

Dale M. Johnson
Dept. of Behavioral Sciences
600 South College
Tulsa, Oklahoma 74104

Appendix G

Cost-Effectiveness of Instructional Systems

How much does it cost for the utilization of a given instructional system? Will the instructional cost index increase or decrease by:

1. Including more students in the program?
2. Using teacher aids in place of regular teachers in certain learning activities?
3. Relieving teachers of some student-contact time and developing additional independent study activities for students?
4. Decreasing some of the required performance levels?

These are questions of educational economics. The complete answers are not yet available. The operating budgets of schools are designed mainly for auditors and not for those who are concerned with day-by-day operations.

The problem of cost-analysis as it relates to instructional systems is that:

1. Costs are seldom linear.
2. Costs records are not adequate if and when they are kept to indicate day-by-day cost of instructional systems.
3. Not all relevant costs appear in the account, therefore making it difficult, if not impossible, to analyze.

The simplest way to measure the cost of an instructional system is to divide the cost of the system by the number of students using it within a given period. Then get the cost-per-student enrollment figure. For example: if it cost $200 to produce and utilize a filmstrip and 200 students used it during a given period, the cost-per-student figure is $1.00.

Another method is to compute the time per week, month, semester, or year that students actually interact with a given system. The formula is:

$$\text{Cost} = \frac{\text{Credit (unit)}}{\text{Class hours/Week}} \text{ x T (Hours) x Enrollment}$$

"Credit" or unit means the number of unit value a student receives for completing the course in question successfully. "T" means the actual time a student spends interacting with the system per week, or in another time span.

The index number itself has no meaning. After the costs for a topic, unit, or course have been assessed it is then necessary to determine whether the operating costs are too high, acceptable or relatively low in comparison to observed outcomes. The calculations should be repeated each time a particular unit, topic, or course is taught so that any change in the cost index can be determined and the reasons for the change evaluated.

Quantitative and analytical methods of determining cost-effectiveness are not always possible when dealing with humans. Therefore, you should recognize the possibilities of using nonquantitative outcomes in determining cost-effectiveness of instructional systems. Observations of the behavior of students, their replies to informational and attitudinal questionnaires, rating scales by students, members of the staff and teachers at the end of unit, topic, or course to determine the degree of success for the system are some other means that may be used to evaluate programs.

There are still other ways to make subjective judgments about cost-effectiveness of instructional systems. Some are: the accomplishments of students in subsequent courses, topics, or units; students' future selection of courses; their vocational and avocational interests in the subject areas that the instructional systems covered; their study habits at a subsequent time; their ability to work independently; and other follow-up studies of students.

Cost decisions must be related to the quality of the instructional system. The above methods do not properly treat such a requirement.

References

The references, which follow, will be of value to those who wish to do further reading in the field and those who are interested in greater details of the topics discussed. Throughout the text certain references were cited using the names of authors only. Below the references are given in more detail.

Designing Instructional Systems

Banathy, Bela, *Instructional Systems* (Belmont, Cal.: Fearon Publishers, 1968).

Briggs, Leslie J., *Handbook of Procedures for the Design of Instruction* (Pittsburgh: American Institute for Research, 1970).

Bruner, J. S., *The Process of Education* (Cambridge, Mass.: Harvard University Press, 1965).

Drumheller, Sidney, *Handbook of Curriculum Design for Individualized Instruction* (Englewood Cliffs, N.J.: Educational Technology Publication, 1971).

Glaser, Robert, "Components of the Instructional Process" (In *Educational Technology,* New York: Holt, Rinehart and Winston, 1964).

Heinich, Robert, *Technology and the Management of Instruction* (Department of Audiovisual Instruction, 1201 16th Street, N.W., Washington, D.C. 20036, 1970).

Kaplan, Abraham, *The Conduct of Inquiry* (San Francisco, Chandler Publishing Company, 1964).

Kemp, Jerrold E., *Instructional Design* (Belmont, Cal.: Fearon Publishers, 1971).

Lessinger, Leon, *Every Kid A Winner: Accountability In Education* (New York: Simon and Schuster, 1970).

Mager, Robert and Kenneth Beach, *Developing Vocational Instruction* (Belmont, Cal.: Fearon Publishers, 1967).

Maritain, Jacques, *Education at the Crossroad* (New Haven, Conn.: Yale University Press, 1968).

Rosner, Benjamin, *The Power of Competency-Based Teacher Education: A Report* (Boston: Allyn and Bacon, Inc., 1972).

Learning Theory

Borger, R. and A. E. Seaborne, *The Psychology of Learning* (Baltimore: Penguin Books, 1966).

Gagné, Robert M., *The Conditions of Learning* (New York: Holt, Rinehart and Winston, 1965).

Glaser, Robert, "Psychological Bases for Instructional Design," A/V *Communication Review,* Winter, 1966, pp. 433-49.

Johnson, Richard and Others, *The Theory and Management of Systems* (New York: McGraw-Hill Company, 1967).

Wiman, Raymond V. and Wesley C. Meierhenry, *Educational Media: Theory Into Practice* (Columbus, Ohio: Charles E. Merrill Publishing Company, 1969).

Learning Objectives

Bloom, Benjamin and Others, *Taxonomy of Educational Objectives, Handbook I: Cognitive Domain* (New York: David McKay, 1956).

Canfield, Albert A., "A Rationale for Performance Objectives," *Audiovisual Instruction,* February, 1968, pp. 127-129.

Gronlund, Norman E., *Stating Behavioral Objectives for Classroom Instruction* (New York: Macmillan, 1970).

Kibler, Robert J. and Others, *Objectives for Instruction and Evaluation* (Boston: Allyn and Bacon, 1974).

Krathwohl, David R. and Others, *Taxonomy of Educational Objectives, Handbook II: Affective Domain* (New York: David McKay, 1964).

Mager, Robert F., *Preparing Instructional Objectives* (Belmont, Cal.: Fearon Publishers, 1962).

Popham, W. James, *Instructional Objectives Exchange* (Los Angeles: University of California at Los Angeles, Graduate School of Education, 1969).

Simpson, Elizabeth Jane, "The Classification of Educational Objectives in the Psychomotor Domain," *The Psychomotor Domain*, Vol. 3, Gryphon House, 1972, pp. 43-56.

Educational Media

Bretz, Rudy, *The Selection of Appropriate Communication Media for Instruction: A Guide for Designers of Air Force Technical Training Programs* (Santa Monica, Cal.: United States Air Force Project Rand, 1971).

Briggs, Leslie J. and Others, *Instructional Media: A Procedure for the Design of Multi-Media Instruction, A Critical Review of the Research, and Suggestions for Future Research* (Washington, D.C.: United States Office of Education, Contract No. OE–5–16–011, October, 1965).

Coger, Richard Mondell, "The Development of a Selection Model and an Effectiveness Model to Assist Teachers in Monitoring the Levels of Accountability of Educational Media," (Unpublished Ph.D. dissertation, The Ohio State University, 1972).

————, "A Model Designed to Determine the Effectiveness of Educational Media," (A presentation at the Second World Council of Comparative Education Societies, Geneva, Switzerland, June 28 - July 2, 1974).

Dale, Edgar, *Audiovisual Methods in Teaching* (3rd Edition, New York: Holt, Rinehart, and Winston, 1969).

Erickson, Carlton, *Administering Instructional Media Programs* (New York: Macmillan, 1968).

Gerlach, Vernon S. and Donald P. Ely, *Teaching and Media: A Systematic Approach* (Englewood Cliffs, N. J.: Prentice-Hall, 1971).

Kemp, Jerrold E., *Planning and Producing Audiovisual Materials* (San Francisco: Chandler, 1968).

McLuhan, Marshall, *Understanding Media: The Extension of Man* (New York: The New American Library, Inc., 1964).

Meierhenry, W. C., *Media Competencies for Teachers* (Washington, D.C.: United States Office of Education, no date).

Tosti, Donald T. and John R. Ball, "A Behavioral Approach to Instructional Design and Media Selection," A/V *Communication Review*, Vol. 17, 1969, pp. 5-25.

Wittich, Walter A. and Charles F. Schuller, *Instructional Technology: Its Nature and Use* (Fifth Edition, New York: Harper & Row, Publishers, 1973).

Evaluation

Metfessel, Newton S. and William B. Michael, "A Paradigm Involving Multiple Criterion Measures for the Evaluation of the Effectiveness of School Programs," *Educational and Psychological Measurement,* Winter, 1967, pp. 931-943.

Provus, Malcolm M., *Evaluation of Ongoing Programs in the Public School System* (Pittsburgh: Pittsburgh Public Schools, 1968).

Scriven, Michael, "The Methodology of Evaluation," *AERA Monograph Series on Curriculum Evaluation* (Washington D.C.: American Educational Research Association, 1967).

Stake, Robert E., "The Countenance of Educational Evaluation," *Teachers College Record,* April, 1967, PP. 523-540.

Stufflebeam, Daniel and Others, *Educational Evaluation and Decision Making* (Phi Delta Kappa National Study Commission on Evaluation, The 11th PDK Symposium on Educational Research, The Ohio State University, 1970).

Thorndike, Robert L. and Elizabeth Hagen, *Measurement and Evaluation in Psychology and Education* (New York: John Wiley and Sons, 1961).

Decision Making

Coombs, Philip H., *The World Educational Crisis: A System Analysis* (New York: Oxford University Press, 1968).

Dettre, John R., *Decision Making in the Secondary School Classroom* (London: Intext Educational Publishers, 1970).

Goulet, R. R., *Educational Change, The Reality and the Promise* (New York: Citation Press, 1968).

Hartley, Harry J., *Educational Planning—Programming—Budgeting—A System Approach* (Englewood Cliffs, N. J.: Prentice-Hall, Inc., 1968).

Heinich, Robert, "Instructional Technology and Instructional Management: A Proposal for a New Theoretical Structure," (Unpublished doctoral dissertation, The University of Southern California, 1967).

Cost-Effectiveness

Miller, James G., "Deciding Whether and How to Use Educational Technology in the Light of Cost-Effectiveness Evaluation," (Washington, D.C.: Academy for Educational Development, Inc., 1970), 49 pp.

Molnar, Andrew, "Media and Cost-Effectiveness," A paper presented at DAVI Convention, Detroit, April 30, 1970, 8 pp.

Speagle, R. E., "Cost—Benefits: A Buyer's Guide for Instructional Technology." A support paper in *To Improve Learning: A Report to the President and the Congress of the United States,* by the Commission on Instructional Technology (Washington, D.C.: Academy of Educational Development, Inc., 1970), 31 pp.

The Cost—Ed Model (Washington, D.C.: Educational Turnkey Systems, Inc., 1971).

"The Cost of Audiovisual Instruction," *School Management,* June, 1964, pp. 81-94.

"The Cost of Audiovisual Instruction," *School Management,* June, 1966, pp. 111-120.

"The Cost of Audiovisual Instruction, 1962 to 1968-69," *School Management,* October, 1968, pp. 67-84.

Facilities and Equipment

DeBernardis, Amo and Others, *Planning Schools for New Media* (Portland, Oregon: Division of Education, Portland State College, 1961).

Green, Alan C.,(ed.), *Educational Facilities With New Media* (Washington, D.C.: National Education Association, 1966).

Mahar, Mary H. (ed.), *The School Library as a Materials Center* (Washington, D.C.: U.S. Office of Education, 1964).

Standards for School Media Programs (Washington, D. C.: American Library Association and National Education Association, 1969).

The Audio-Visual Equipment Directory (annual publication), National Audio-Visual Association, 3150 Spring Street, Fairfax, Virginia 22030.

Miscellaneous

Born, David G., *Instructor Manual for Development of a Personalized Instruction Course* (Salt Lake City: University of Utah, Center to Improve Learning and Instruction, 1970).

Burns, Richard W. and Gary D. Brooks (eds.), *Curriculum Design in a Changing Society* (Englewood Cliffs, N. J.: Educational Technology Publication, 1970).

Cay, Donald F., *Curriculum Design for Learning* (New York: Bobbs-Merrill Company, Inc., 1966).

Deterline, William A., *An Introduction to Programmed Instruction* (Englewood Cliffs, N.J.: Prentice-Hall, 1962).

Holt, John, *How Children Fail?* (New York: Pitman Publishing Corporation, 1964).

Howes, Virgil M., *Individualization of Instruction: A Teaching Strategy* (New York: Macmillan, 1970).

Hunter, Madeline, "Waiting Time Becomes Learning Time," *Instructor,* November, 1973.

Mager, R. F., *Developing Attitude Toward Learning* (Palo Alto, Cal.: Fearon Publishers, 1968).

Silberman, C.E., *Crisis in the Classroom* (New York: Random House, 1970).

Tyler, R. W., *Basic Principles of Curriculum and Instruction* (Chicago: The University of Chicago Press, 1950).

Trow, Wm. Clark, *Paths to Educational Reform* (Englewood Cliffs, N.J.: Prentice-Hall, 1970).